VARIETIES OF INTERPRETATION

Joseph Anthony Mazzeo

VARIETIES OF INTERPRETATION

UNIVERSITY OF NOTRE DAME PRESS

NOTRE DAME   LONDON

Library of Congress Cataloging in Publication Data

Mazzeo, Joseph Anthony, 1923–
    Varieties of interpretation.

    Bibliography: p.
    Includes index.
    1. Hermeneutics. I. Title.
BD241.M33   220.6′3   78-51518
ISBN 0-268-00589-3

Contents

Acknowledgments

THE BULK OF THE FIFTH ESSAY first appeared in *Thought* under the essay title in 1976, and the substance of third essay appeared under the title "Allegorical Interpretation and History" in *Comparative Literature in 1978*. I would like to thank the editors of both journals for publishing some of my work in earlier versions and for their kind permission to use it here.

Preface

I CAN BEST DESCRIBE this book as a set of reflections on some of those recurrent and crucial occasions in cultural history when acts of interpretation are not simply required but demanded. Every culture possesses texts generally regarded as indispensable to its system of knowledge and its structure of values. While the texts remain "fixed," the processes of cultural and social change alter the context of interpretation and render the texts less and less immediately available to understanding, or may even place existent texts in radical contradiction to new values or knowledge which have come with the passage of time. A crucial conflict then arises between the imperative need to preserve the indispensable text and the new criteria of truth and morality which contradict much or all of the apparent meaning of the text. Clearly, the parade example of such a cultural conflict is provided by the history of biblical exegesis, but secular works of literature and art, legal codes, and political constitutions recurrently present the historian of thought with similar instances of the "demand" for interpretation. Much, if not all, of the history of philosophy could be written in terms of the response of great thinkers to cultural crises calling for the reinterpretation of sacred or normative texts and the requisite creation of new methods of interpretation. Plato, St. Augustine, Spinoza, Heidegger immediately come to mind and other examples would not be hard to find. In this respect, my subject is unbounded, so I have permitted myself to range widely at the expense of having a single focus.

Thus the reader will find discussions of biblical exegesis, the Platonic view of myth, modern and classical views of allegory, the relation between religious and scientific thought, and of the interpretive methods of modern existentialistists and structuralists. He will, on the other hand, find few interpretive discussions in the way that a literary critic, for example, might address himself to specific texts, the history of their interpretation, or the special interpretive problems a particular work might present. My concern has been to illuminate a recurrent cultural situation of fundamental importance for our understanding of cultural change and its consequences, although I have tried to indicate how my subject may help clarify what we do when we make acts of interpretation.

This book, moreover, is the outcome of reflection upon previous studies of a more specialized character. If we were living in an earlier century, I might have tried a more ample description of its contents in the title itself, a title which might have run like this: "Sundry and Various Reflections on the Hermeneutical Art," together with "Further Reflections on the Occasions which Elicit Acts of Interpretation, Their Necessity, Purpose and Utility." But such titles are no longer in vogue and must be introduced almost covertly, as I have just done. I have not, therefore, written a formal treatise on what European scholars are more likely than Americans to call "hermeneutics." We have a number of distinguished treatises on the subject, from Schleiermacher to the works of E. D. Hirsch and Emilio Betti, and I have tried to make full use of them.

A glance at my table of contents should indicate more clearly than anything else what I have tried to do. Two of the essays deal specifically with the most demanding subjects of interpretation, myth and allegory. Whether we seek to understand the myths of living religions or those myths of ancient structures of belief that have passed into our cultural legacy, here as nowhere else the peculiar problems as well as the ingenuity and cultural resources demanded of the interpreter are clearly revealed. Only allegory compares with myth in this respect. I have drawn a careful distinction between works constructed to be read as allegories and works we may choose to read as allegories even if not so constructed. In either case, the resources of the exegete are often pushed to the limits, whether he imputes allegorical meanings to the text or "unpacks" the allegorical meanings in it. These two essays are intended as case histories wherein both the achievements and absurdities of interpreters are rendered intelligible, instances in which what interpreters do is writ large.

My model for the analysis of allegory as a principle of construction derives from a study of biblical typology and its influence. That influence served to generate a "style" which interprets reality in a new modality. If the biblical paratactic style evokes a portentous background for events, and the hypotactic style illuminates the foreground of events—to take Auerbach's magisterial analysis as a point of departure—the allegorical "style" locates events as simultaneously pointing to past and present, to objective and subjective realities. Typological interpretations of the Old Testament and typological constructions in the New Testament conferred an utterly new potentiality on the ancient rhetorical device of personification. It became the device through which the author could construct a new story which also retells an old paradigmatic story at the same time as the narrative refers to spiritual events or the events of consciousness. From another point of view, we may describe constructed allegory as presenting us with an explicit text which makes visible both an implicit older text and a "psychological" one.

Three of the remaining essays in the book deal, respectively, with the historical situations in which the need for interpretation becomes pronounced (if not always acute), with a writer's style as itself an interpretive activity, and with the function of interpretation in mediating the processes of cultural change. In these essays I have allowed myself to engage in some large generalizations and speculations. I have, for example, drawn some rather extensive parallels between biological and cultural change in my attempt to describe the cultural function of interpretation, parallels which biologists and anthropologists would find too "unscientific," and perhaps rightly so. I do not pass beyond the point of inviting my reader to view cultural change and biological change as analogous in the light of the model furnished by information theory. This is simply a way of asking my reader to entertain a different view of familiar activities which may call attention to aspects of them not previously noticed.

Similarly, in my first chapter, the problem of how historical and cultural "distance" generates the need for interpretation is implicitly viewed in terms of the model furnished by the concept of entropy: cultural change diminishes our access to the "information" of a text and interpretation is the "work" done to restore both information and access.

While we may say that interpretation substitutes one text for another, such a formulation is obviously too crude as it stands. The interpreter's text has the function of preserving the original and must therefore stand in an ordered metaphorical and analogical relationship to it. This relationship may be described as "negentropy," the creation of greater semantic order where cultural change and historical distance have increased the semantic entropy of the text. When Wordsworth described the function of poetry as rendering the commonplace uncommon, as "making it new," he was describing how the poet reverses the loss of meaning which habit, "getting and spending," contributes to the wasting of our powers. The task of the interpreter is not very different, from this point of view, for the interpreter mediates and slows down the processes of cultural change by recreating meaning.

If we give to the idea of interpretation its widest possible latitude, then it is something we do all the time, even in our sleep, in this psychological age, with the very stuff of dreams. The shape itself of our utterances is interpretive, and so I have devoted the second essay to the question of style as interpretation. In this essay, my main guides have been Vico and the greatest of his successors among students of literature, Erich Auerbach. If I have recapitulated much that may be familiar, it is only because I would not know how to proceed beyond Auerbach's accomplishment.

Like language or symbolism, interpretation conceived of as a subject for study is unbounded. I cannot pretend to have given an up-to-date account of myth, or allegory, or of theories of interpretation *eo nomine*. Nor have I attempted to cite all the sides on controverted questions, or even all the scholars and critics who have instructed me. I have striven for breadth rather than depth and have allowed myself to be more reflective than "informative" in some restricted sense of that term. I nevertheless hope that I have not been superficial. The teacher will still find E. D. Hirsch's *Validity in Interpretation* unexcelled for his purposes, while the student of Dante or Chaucer will receive far more specifically grounded guidance in the problem of allegory from the works of D. W. Robertson (*Preface to Chaucer*) or Robert Hollander (*Allegory in Dante's Commedia*) than I have attempted to give.

To mention the word "myth" these days is to inaugurate a cycle of debate which could only be stopped by the voice from the whirlwind. My discussion of this subject is in terms of the literary and philosophical tradition of myth and its uses, and therefore limited to the Platonic context. My use of the term myth, a more ample account of what the Platonic context is and why it is comprehensive, I will leave to my text. At this point, I will retreat to a very conventional definition and say that myths are stories about gods and heroes, stories which had, or have, an authoritative, exemplary, and normative function in a culture. The culture to which I address myself is our own, and the two great bodies of myth are biblical and classical.

While I am aware that myth has by no means an exclusively religious or moral-imaginative function, that function which literature has generally been assumed to possess, Plato did pose the terms in which we must deal with our mythic-religious inheritance, at least insofar as that inheritance was largely framed and shaped by imaginative writers, by poets, and by prophets with the gifts of poets.

I will accept for the purpose of my discussion Plato's virtual identification of myth and poetry. Plato's critique of poets in the *Republic* is not, like that of Hobbes or Bacon, for example, an attack on metaphor or figurative expression altogether, but an attack on a corpus of prestigious stories and their implicit claim to morality and truthful representation of reality. Plato thus amalgamates poetry and myth, while a modern interpreter might place them at opposite ends of the expressive possibilities of language. The following passage from Lévi-Strauss' *Structural Anthropology* (p. 206) is illuminating in this regard:

> A remark can be introduced at this point which will help to show the originality of myth in relation to other linguistic phenomena. Myth is the part of language where

the formula *traduttore, tradittore* [translator equals traitor]
reaches its lowest truth value. From that point of view it
should be placed in the gamut of linguistic expressions at
the end opposite to that of poetry, in spite of all the claims
which have been made to prove the contrary. Poetry is a
kind of speech which cannot be translated except at the
cost of serious distortions; whereas the mythical value of
the myth is preserved even through the worst translation.
Whatever our ignorance of the language and the culture of
the people where it originated, a myth is still felt as a myth
by any reader anywhere in the world. Its substance does
not lie in its style, its original music, or its syntax, but in
the *story* which it tells. Myth is language functioning on an
especially high level where meaning succeeds practically
at "taking off" from the linguistic ground on which it
keeps on rolling.

Plato might well have agreed with these observations concerning the difference between myth and poetry, but I don't
think it would have affected the essentials of his analysis, for
the problem of the moral value of myth is set side by side with
the metaphysical problem of the truth value of any literary
mimesis of reality. I should confess that I have found some
modern conceptions of myth far too encompassing to be illuminating for my purposes. In a debate with Sartre, for example,
Lévi-Strauss considered all historical truth merely a set of variations composed by individuals upon themes provided them by
their personal mythologies. To frame what I wished to discuss
socially, in terms of the polytypic definitions of myth to be
found in some of our leading contemporary mythographers,
would have been impossible.

The problematic of myth is that of religious "truth" and of
poetic "fiction." That the concept of myth may be extended in
other directions is undeniable, but for the student of our literary and cultural tradition the Platonic questions may still be the
most important: what truths are given to us in myth? What are
we to make of authoritative but immoral myths? Is mythical
expression autonomous and irreducible to any other kind of
thought? Is myth "primitive" in some pejorative sense of that
word? Can we, should we, transcend it altogether, or is it necessary if we are to understand at all?

To the degree that myth, in both its covert and overt forms, plays its important role in modern Western societies, then the questions framed in the Platonic tradition of mythical interpretation are surely important even if anthropologists have other questions to ask of the function of myth in the societies they study. These questions are fundamentally none other than those the theologian or the humanistic scholar asks of the texts he studies. They are the inevitable questions we must ask in societies in which the historical consciousness has been developed. Insofar as civilized people transcend custom they must question myth, while insofar as they are governed by custom they are free to possess myth directly.

In short, the civilized person must be the interpreter of myth whether he will or no, for myths have become problematic for him in quite the same way that the Greek legacy became problematic for Plato: vital traditions framed in the language of myth and story and conveyed in works of high religious and poetic authority demand their conservation at the same time that they pose great questions. Awareness of historical distance often enters a culture in just this way. The data of the past lose some of their contemporanity but must still be used to illuminate the problems of the present. The traditional stories may then be rejected, replaced, or subsumed into a fresh network of analogies. Single vision, which Blake deplored in Newton, is no longer possible and must be replaced by a kind of double vision in which tradition is viewed under the aegis of the present.

My final chapter on myth and science in the theology of Rudolf Bultmann is a modern example of a typical and acute instance of an interpretive or exegetical crisis. The believing theologian confronts a mythological and poetic text to which he imputes an overriding authority equipped with faith, in some sense of that word, but clearly committed to taking full account of modern scientific and historical criteria of truth concerning nature and historical events. The literary critic may be allowed to rest in a theory of fiction, but there is a necessity imposed on the theologian, which his secular counterpart may avoid, to proclaim truth of unique and universal significance. Precisely because of this, the humanist may be instructed by the theologian's methods and results.

Over the time this book was in progress I benefitted greatly from numerous informal conversations with my colleagues and students in the Department of English and Comparative Literature at Columbia and at Princeton during my tenure there as Senior Fellow of the Council of the Humanities. This may account for the conversational character of some parts of this book, a quality which I hope is not without advantages.

Interpretation and Its Occasions

Traditional ideas are never static. They are either fading into meaningless formulae, or are gaining power by new lights thrown by a more delicate apprehension. They are transformed by the urge of critical reason, by the vivid evidence of emotional experience, and by the cold certainties of scientific perception. One fact is certain, you cannot keep them still.

Alfred North Whitehead
Science and the Modern World *(1926)*

THE TWENTIETH CENTURY has been called the "Age of Anxiety" and probably with considerable justice, but if we were to seek a single rubric to describe the intellectual life of the last century we would have to call it the "Age of Exegesis." Even the progress of the sciences can be subsumed under this description. Different models or paradigms of method and interpretation play a critical role in directing the course of research. The same physical phenomena may be interpreted in terms of particles and forces, or in terms of fields. Light, in some of its behavior, must be understood as a wave motion and, in other instances, as constituted of particles.

Certainly, the existence of alternate and valid ways of interpreting physical phenomena does not compromise the solid results of scientific research, but it does raise problems of interpretation. The quantum physicist may use matrix algebra and wave mechanical formulations with relative indifference, since both formulations are isomorphic and both permit him to interpret physical data. The fact that an electron may be viewed as a charged particle, or a charged cloud, or even as the area under a curve, that it may be imagined as a "solid" point or a "disturbance" spreading out in a region of space, simply means that the scientist has moved a little closer to the exegete confronted with a plurality of valid interpretations of his text.

The book of nature is surely written in mathematical language, as Galileo argued, but mathematics is a far more complex language than Galileo thought and will become even more complex than it is now. The visualizable geometrical figures which Galileo assumed were nature's vocabulary have been replaced by a language of relations, a language of order, which may be comprehended but not, in a material way, imagined.[1] Euler's astonishing theorem which relates the trigonometric and exponential functions, two apparently totally different conceptions, and the invention of non-Euclidean geometries marked the end of "literalism" in physical science insofar as science would find uses, as it has, for such mathematical innovations. We shall have occasion to refer to the great differences between acts of interpretation of natural phenomena and the exegesis of artistic and humanistic texts, but we may for the moment reflect that the concept of interpretation has entered into scientific thought in a way not totally unfamiliar to the humanist.[2]

Nature requires interpretation because its operations are hidden. What we see is not, in some sense, what is "really" going on. Francis Bacon was profoundly right when he said that nature, through experiment, must be "put to the torture" if we are to make it yield its secrets. Certainly, much scientific advance has been propelled by nonobvious reinterpretations of the obvious. It is not obvious that species change, or that the "norm" of motion is inertial, or that, in the absence of friction, all objects fall to the ground, whatever their mass, at the same rate of acceleration. Nor is it obvious that the earth is not the appropriate center for the analysis of planetary motions. In some respects, the scientific interpreter is like the ancient allegorist who found all sorts of astonishing significances utterly different from the surface meaning of a text—but with considerably more justification to be sure.

As the occasions for the interpretation of nature arise from the hiddenness of its causes and operations, so the need for the interpretation of literature, philosophy, religion, and art arises from the alienness conferred by historicity—the cultural changes which occur over time in our own civilization—or the sheer foreignness of an alien culture.[3]

All that has happened within Western civilization since the Renaissance, for example, has rendered Dante's *Divine Comedy* to some degree foreign to us, in spite of the continuities that the cultural historian might find between Dante's time and our own. Generations of readers have found it worth the study, to be sure, but Dante's wish to give us in his poem the *omne scibile,* the whole of the knowable world, can reach us only as a magnificent intention. It is precisely the cosmology and theology of the poem that we must study as literary archeologists in order to discover and assimilate its literary value.

It is surprising how few aestheticians have been as candid as R. G. Collingwood about our relation to the artistic and humanistic past.

> We are all, though many of us are snobbish enough to wish to deny it, in far closer sympathy with the art of the music-hall and picture-palace than with Chaucer and Cimabue, or even Shakespeare and Titian. By an effort of historical sympathy we can cast our minds back into the art of a remote past or an alien present, and enjoy the carvings of cavemen and Japanese colour-prints; but the possibility of this effort is bound up with that development of historical thought which is the greatest achievement of our civilization in the last two centuries, and it is utterly impossible to people in whom this development has not taken place. The natural and primary aesthetic attitude is to enjoy contemporary art, to despise and dislike the art of the recent past, and wholly to ignore everything else.[4]

Those of us to whom higher education has been made available are perhaps brought to the threshold of the kind of historical imagination Collingwood speaks of, but without such preparation Cimabue and Chaucer do remain in some degree remote, although not as impervious to our understanding as the myths of those South American Indians so ingeniously interpreted by Lévi-Strauss. There are some slender but strong threads of continuity with the Middle Ages that do not tie us to the Indians. Nor should we forget that an art which possessed a recognizable religious and social content remains more accessible than a contemporary art which is experimental or innovative. It is far more likely that the hypothetical man in the street would find Chaucer's *Troilus* an enjoyable and instructive work than Joyce's *Ulysses* and that he would perform his devotions before a Cimabue rather than a Dali. There is a large measure of truth in Collingwood's view of the role of the historical imagination, but the remoteness of *Finnegans Wake* or of the more difficult poems of Wallace Stevens obviously cannot be attributed to the passage of time and historical change. They are written to require a great deal of effort to be read and must remain caviar to the general at any time.

Whether the acts of understanding and interpretation we bring to primitive but contemporary cultures should be viewed as analogous to acts of the historical imagination is open to some question. There is, however, no doubt that similar acts of the mind must be brought to bear on works that are alien in a cultural space, so to speak, as to works that are alien in time, even if ancestral of our present. It is hard to imagine the brilliant interpretive achievements of a Boas, a Malinowski, or a Lévi-Strauss without the magnificent historical reconstructions of Greece, Rome, and the Middle Ages which were the result of eighteenth- and nineteenth-century historical scholarship. What is required by both anthropologists and exegetes of humanistic and historical texts is the capacity to perceive the validity of looking at the world in ways other than those we find familiar. A feel for the coherence of unfamiliar metaphorical and analogical possibilities is the presupposition of all interpretation, whatever the conditions which make a text or a work of art remote.

What appears as primitive or temporally remote must be understood as different but coherent. In this sense, historical and cultural perspectivism has rendered the notion of the primitive or the "archeological" very ambiguous indeed. A culture, or the metaphorical system of a text, is viewed as a kind of Kantian a priori, as the structure of categories through which the whole is glimpsed. With the death of naive realism we cannot easily assume a kind of hard-rock truth which may serve as a ready reference for what is archaic or "savage." Any reality is interpreted reality, a particular symbolic construct which reveals and hides different attributes of both self and world. Although modern science is too diversified and complex an enterprise to yield a world-view, a hard-rock truth, when we refer nowadays to various phenomena as archaic, superstitious, primitive, or what have you, we seem to be contrasting them to the characteristic procedures we use in making a scientific technological and industrial society work. Rationality and modernity are thus viewed as synonymous with the efficient adaptation of ends to means, with the operational value of concepts and, too often, in terms of a naive pragmatism.

Lévi-Strauss, in his *La pensée sauvage*,[5] has made it abundantly clear that the tribal societies he has studied are extraordinarily coherent from the logical point of view. They, too, adapt means to ends. Peoples once thought to be "primitive" or "savage" are capable of the most differentiated classification of animals and plants, for example, although their differentia may at first seem arbitrary or elusive to Westerners. While the classification "mammal" may be unintelligible to them, they may find a single classification for the most diverse types of animals according to similar feeding habits, a classification profoundly significant and functionally more useful. The manner in which such views of the natural world's categories are immediately applied to the social or cultural world in primitive societies does not make those societies any easier to understand. Yet when we reflect on how technology is interposed between us and a more immediate perception both of nature and of the basic cultural tasks which sustain life, we see how sensible it may really be to view culture and nature as mirroring each other.

In a culture where the major technological achievement is the hollowing of tree trunks to make canoes or drums, all hollowed objects, natural or artificial, easily achieve a privileged relationship to one another. Even we, when we think of the brain as a computer, we may be saying more about the way we want to "cut up" reality than about either the brain or computers. Similitudes between objects may, in fact, be drawn at many tangents, and the strangeness of some may yield when we grasp how different peoples must deal with the constraints of their existence and how those constraints focus attention on particular aspects of their environment we have no reason to notice. A man who fears cats may seek to avoid them, but he will surely notice any cat that appears on his horizon.

The metaphorical or analogical process is perhaps the master key to interpretation, far more important than the study of symbolism as such. In fact, one does not need to be too conversant with the literature on the symbolic interpretation of dreams or myth to realize that when an author succeeds in persuading us of a symbol's meaning he has usually explained it as a metaphor which has been rendered abstract and independent of its analogical character. Most symbols, if not all, would seem to be deracinated metaphors.

Aristotle thought, in the *Poetics,* that the ability to make apt metaphors and draw revealing similitudes was a mark of genius, and so indeed it is, if we understand the process as the discernment of resemblances. Moreover, a metaphor is not simply a similitude between two objects but is the linguistic process by which we relate ourselves to the world and either make or discard identifications. Metaphor making begins with language itself, and it is through discerning differences and similitudes that the growing child clarifies the relationships between subject and objects. Through predicating metaphorical relations, he brings wider and wider ranges of brute experience into the realm of consciousness. Since the acquisition of identity is, moreover, under the dominion of desires and fears, the metaphorical process is also the neurotic process, insofar as contradictory images and identifications may simultaneously enter the one psyche. We may not be successful in assuming the identity we desire or in fleeing from the one we fear, or we may both desire and fear a single identity.[6]

So natural is this metaphorical process, so vital to the formation of the human being, that unified cultures are largely lacking in exegetes, in the sense that they do not have interpreters who might step outside their network of correspondences and verify or deny *our* interpretations. Some kind of cultural pluralism would seem to be indispensable in generating the need to interpret and understand what we mean by what we do and think. Only in a world in which it is possible to deny one truth in the name of another, or one value in the name of an opposing one, does the mediatory function of exegesis become a necessity. What I have called the "Age of Exegesis" has as well been the age of rapid social and cultural change. Photographs, recordings, films, relatively inexpensive means of publication, travel, and all the rest have created a vast "museum without walls," to use the phrase of Malraux, not only an art museum but also a museum of history, natural history and ethnography. Every time and every place can now be present to us for an exegetical onslaught.

Just having to understand so much compounds the normal uncertainties of interpretation. Absolute certainty, whatever that might really mean, is not possible even with a text or a practice within our own immediate culture. We can, however, ask that our interpretations be valid. To do this is simply to affirm that all men are involved in the metaphorical process, that they share common needs, hopes, wishes, and fears and that we can trust the work of understanding as it subsumes larger and larger areas of experience into a more comprehensive and unified structure of meaning. Understanding is, from this point of view, identical with the metaphorical process itself. We understand a figure by incorporating it into a more inclusive figure, so that a number of particulars are brought under the rule of a class. Since all categories of class are categories of similitude, our class categories will have some degree of validity. But since any group of particulars may resemble each other in different ways, no class is absolute except as defined with utter precision in respect to a similitude.

A perceived similitude, however strange, represents a focus of interest, a desire or fear, an intention or purpose, even a practical necessity. Above all, it is the presupposition or occasion of an act. Einstein said of scientists if you would understand them don't ask them what they are doing but watch them. In the sphere of culture, we can ask and then ponder what is said in relation to what is done.

Interpretation, for most of its history, was the interpretation of content. An obscure meaning was read in the light of a similar meaning taken to be clearer and a new figure similar to the old replaced it in the understanding. In modern times, exegesis has taken some new and striking directions. It may be true that there is no utterly new way of interpreting and that we may find precedents for Freud or the structuralists or the existentialists somewhere among the writings of the ancients, but precedent cannot eclipse the richness and magnitude and complexity of modern exegetical movements. Freud as exegete gives a new and compelling version of an old distinction between the latent and the manifest meaning of a "text," whether dream, myth, or symptom. Freud's two levels of meaning are related to two psychic systems, governed by a different "syntax" of meaning and with entirely different relations to consciousness.

The structuralists are most conspicuously represented by Lévi-Strauss, and here we find a method of analysis which, in principle, ignores overt content. Although in practice Lévi-Strauss gives more attention to content than he would theoretically allow, he views myth essentially as a code and myth makers as unconscious of what they are doing. Myths come into being as presentations of the polarities of experience, as the attempt to mediate oppositions. This meaning or intention of myth is not to be found in the narrative as such, or any of its variants taken singly. It is, on the contrary, found in the structure of myth, structure revealed upon analysis of all possible versions of the myth however incompatible they may be with each other in detail. The elements of myth—representations of "high" and "low," male and female, raw and cooked foods, and so on—are isolated from the text and arranged sequentially with an analysis of how the movement of the surface narrative, however strange or illogical, mediates oppositions and polarities of experience. The great polarity which finally incorporates all the oppositions of myth and governs its structure is the polarity of nature and culture.

Existentialism, in the person of Heidegger, marked a break with the exegetical tradition of the past in denying the assumption that any act of exegesis was essentially concerned with ascertaining authorial intention. However absurd some of the ancient allegorizations of Homer may seem, the old interpreters were surely convinced that the poet intended the meanings they read into him. Hans-Georg Gadamer, Rudolf Bultmann, and others in the existential tradition of exegesis feel no such constraint. They are as free to set aside the question of authorial intent as Lévi-Strauss is to set aside the overt content of the myths he analyzes.

In a way, Freud is the father, acknowledged or not, of these latter two movements in interpretation, for they both appeal to "unintended" meanings. Behind existentialism there is, of course, the specter of a radical historicism that makes all understanding of the past so strictly a function of the present state of consciousness that it is impossible, in principle, to ask and answer an apparently simple question like: what did Plato mean in this passage? In different ways and with different degrees of validity, existentialist, structuralist, and psychoanalyst readily go against what the text apparently means. For Freud, the unconscious system speaks through the overt meaning; for Lévi-Strauss, the "structure" of mind speaks through the surface of myth; for Heidegger, "being" speaks through language.

Such principles of exegesis cannot be applied without some measure of contradiction. Freud escapes inconsistency by positing two kinds of mental processes, each with its own "language," syntax, and function: the primary and the secondary process, more or less related to the system of conscious and preconscious on the one hand and to unconscious on the other. Heidegger and Lévi-Strauss do not, it seems to me, solve certain contradictions. If with Heidegger we take the position of radical historicism and deny the necessity or possibility of determining authorial intent, how can we affirm that our existentialist interpretation does in fact go against some explicit meaning of the text? With the structuralists, how can we ignore the obvious narrative of the myth as content, while having to understand that same narrative as content in order to determine how the various oppositions expressed in it are mediated? Can we claim to ignore the overt content of myth while arranging that content into binary patterns presumed to constitute a fundamental code revealing the structure of mind?

One need not pursue the problems of theory in these exegetical systems to realize that what they do have in common, despite their differences, is that they seek meaning in a deeper structure of a "text" than is immediately discernible. This is true even if the text in question is not universally viewed as puzzling or problematic. After all, fundamentalist readers of the Bible have no problem swallowing the text whole, the Navahos scarcely need anthropologists to tell them what they are doing with their myths, and some dreamers are singularly uninterested in their dreams even if they ought to be.[7]

Modern science, as we shall see, has helped engender the need for new exegetical methods and has done so in different ways. Cherished old beliefs must be reinterpreted if they are to be preserved. The claims of art and religion to offering a kind of truth cannot be advanced without a good deal of specification concerning the kind of truths thus offered. Most important, perhaps, is the fact that, largely as the effect of scientific thought, modern culture views the truth as emerging out of the future and not as enshrined in traditions or documents of the past. By a strange irony, the very capacity that modern historical and scientific thought has created to understand the past has in some respects served to make the past seem, in some quarters at least, something substantially transcended.

If, within Western civilization, we were to seek one text on which virtually all the characteristic problems of interpretation can be brought to bear we would have to choose the Bible. It is remote from us in time even though a copy of it can be found in any hotel room in the United States; much of it is "primitive" enough to interest the anthropologist and archeologist; it represents some of the greatest literature we possess; it has had, of course, an incalculable influence on Western thought and culture. But the Bible is of special interest to us because it is the only book which can command the widest possible range of readers from the barely literate to the most highly trained. It is also unique in being the only book systematically made accessible, even to the illiterate, through preaching. Hence its metaphors and myths are apprehended in the most diverse possible ways, literally and symbolically, and its interpretations range from the pitiless literalism of the hell fire preacher to the existential insights of Bultmannian demythologizers.

To be sure, the Bible has demanded exegesis generation

after generation, but the occasions for exegesis have been surprisingly different. The early Christians, for example, confronted the problem of what relationship they were to have to the Old Testament, a book which was surely sacred but full of cultic and ritual ordinances which were not binding on them. In essence this problem turned on the question of the "newness" of Christianity. A classic solution was to treat the Old Testament as a typologically prophetic book, prophetic of Christ even in its cultic and ritual statements. This solution demanded an extraordinary exegetical technique, one which would convincingly turn historical events, the practices and beliefs of a religion believed to be transcended, into prophetic ciphers of the messianic fulfillment. The continuity of Christians with their ancestral religion could thus be preserved while they were free to rejoice in their own claim that revelation was fulfilled in them.[8]

But not all Christian exegesis was conservative, as we can see if we turn to some of the Gnostic interpreters of Scripture. Harnack called Gnosticism the extreme hellenization of Christianity, and although this position has been modified by subsequent scholarship, there is a large measure of truth in it. A typical hellenic solution to the problem of Judaism and its sacred texts in relation to Christianity was advanced by the Greek Gnostic Marcion. The Old Testament, in his view, was to be rejected altogether as the revelation of an essentially evil God. The Father of Jesus and the Yahweh of Scripture were not the same God at all. Like a true Hellene of his time, Marcion found the anthropomorphic traits of the divinity displayed in the Old Testament, including his undoubted ferocity, unbefitting the divine nature. Jesus reveals a God totally other than the God hitherto taken to be the true God. Yahweh exists to be sure, but he is evil and presides over an evil universe. Christianity is thus a religion of escape from an evil cosmos run by malevolent powers. Marcion was prepared to eliminate even those parts of the New Testament which he viewed as reflecting this Old Testament conception of the divine nature.

Most hellenizers of Judaism and Christianity, however, were able to make their peace with the sacred texts, new and old. Philo Judaeus and later Origen, Jew and Christian, found in allegorical interpretation a way of harmonizing Scripture with Greek philosophical and moral conceptions of the divine nature. God becomes more impassive, more transcendent, less given to wrath, more universal. Indeed, he comes to be more like Plato's Good than like the vivid omnipresent person we find in the Pentateuch. Both intellectual and moral concerns prompted allegorical exegesis, and the moral concern affected all interpreters of Scripture regardless of their philosophical views.

Ethical monotheism possesses two powerful tendencies which have frequently clashed in its history and which fostered allegorical interpretation. On the one hand, God is good and the source of all good. The universe is governed by a moral order which is revealed by God and understood by man. On the other hand, ethical monotheism views God as a personal will and as omnipotent. The conviction of his absolute sovereignty may lead the believer up to attributing all events, good and evil, to the omnipotent exercise of the divine will. While the primitive believer may well adore a God to whom he attributes all kinds of behavior he would find culpable in his neighbor, a more sensitive ethical nature cannot do so. The absolute will of God must somehow be reconciled with what ethical insight knows to be the morally good. Thus John Stuart Mill advanced the concept of a God limited in power in order to preserve his goodness while Calvin, insisting on the sovereignty of God, swelled the register of those predestined to eternal torment.

How, moreover, was one to interpret a divine command to stone to death a man for picking up sticks on the sabbath? How was one to interpret an Old Testament command to stone an adultress alongside the New Testament example of forgiveness? What was one to make of acts of incest, or suicide, on the part of a hero of sacred history? One might view such harsh or immoral passages as relics of a transcended age, as applicable to a particular situation then but now forbidden. Revelation has, in this view, "increased" to the point where we now know that God does not intend such severe punishment for adultery. Suicide may have been appropriate for Samson in order to fulfill his role in some imperfectly understood divine plan, but we now know that it is not appropriate for the rest of humanity.

The perpetuation of Israel may have depended on incest at one point, but we surely know that incest is forbidden to man in the normal run of things. An event repugnant to a later moral consciousness may also be simply allegorized away and its true significance placed in the allegorical meaning even if it did actually occur. Samson is one type of Christ, and treated as such, even at the expense of ignoring any moral dilemmas his life might present when examined in detail.

Interpretation might thus be demanded on prophetic grounds, a "higher" religious form assimilating and domesticating its "lower" predecessors while retaining continuity with them. Or it might involve taking the mythological and anthropomorphic features of the sacred text and interpreting them allegorically in order to "discover" philosophical truths. This latter tendency was especially strong in the hellenized Christian or Jewish intellectual, for to such a man religion had to present itself in great part as a philosophic system, an assumption quite alien to the original Jewish or Christian believers.[9]

Of course, these different motives in interpretation are not to be found in pure form. Moralizing interpretations of Scripture prompted by ethical repugnance were mixed with philosophical assumptions concerning the divine attributes. Typological interpretations of the Old Testament text were frequently motivated by moral concerns as well as prophetic ones. Sometimes, exegesis was motivated simply by the need to make a puzzling text intelligible. Medieval exegesis abounds in quite extravagant and startling interpretations of texts which today we would understand as historically conditioned statements and consult the archeologist, the anthropologist, and the historian for their meanings. When Dante, in *Purgatorio*, laments that Pope Boniface cannot lead mankind on its proper path because he confounds the temporal and the spiritual, the poet says, "The shepherd who leads may chew the cud but does not have divided hoofs" (16. 98–99). We may, forgivably, be startled to find this meaning derived from cultic ordinances in Lev. 11:3 and Deut. 14:7, "Whatsoever parteth the hoof and cheweth the cud, among the beasts, that shall ye eat. The camel and the hare and the coney chew the cud, but divide not the hoof, therefore they are unclean to you."[10]

Virtually all of the exegetical techniques applied to the Bible were intended to be conservative, to "save the text," as indeed were the allegorical techniques applied by the pagan Greeks to Homer or Hesiod. As the ancient astronomers took as their commandment the injunction to "save the phenomena," to explain the apparent motions of the heavenly bodies as consonant with "perfect" circular symmetries which were not apparent, so the allegorizers, pagan and Christian alike, sought a meaning more suitable to the divine nature wherever the text appeared inconsonant with that nature.

An "enlightened" age found many of the classical myths literally immoral, or subrational, and preferred to blink the frequently improper behavior of the Zeus of Homeric myth and think of him as a symbol of Stoic universal reason. Biblical interpreters were under no less a constraint in interpreting some episodes and practices in their book. While some of the interpretations of classical myth or biblical episodes can strike the modern reader as hopelessly willful, they had the function of preserving indispensable cultural traditions, vital forms of life—and furnished to contemporary philosophical ideas a distinguished and ancient pedigree. Homer or Moses really knew the truth we now know in a different way, and these ancient stories were really symbolic expressions of a single philosophical and moral truth. However unworthy of credence they might appear to be, they were, properly understood, worthy of reverence and philosophically sound to boot.

There were crucial differences between the pagan and Christian allegorizers and interpreters, but both shared the motive of saving the text. There is, as we have seen, among Christian exegetes one exception to the conservative intention of interpretation. While among some of the Gnostics the intention of the interpreter was to subvert the text, Marcion bluntly condemned the whole of the Old Testament as well as some of the New, as a revelation of an evil creator God. This Gnostic took the ferocious injunctions of which Yahweh is capable and the dubious morality of some of the leading personages of the Bible at their face value. Marcion thus subverts and overturns the traditional pieties and evaluations of good and evil held by orthodox interpreters, Jewish or Christian, of the Sacred Text.

In a way, he simply does away with the enormous work of saving the text through allegorical interpretation and between the contradictions of old and new chooses in favor of a narrowly defined notion of the new.[11]

It is hard to find a parallel to the subversive interpretation of Marcion applied to a secular text, although virtually every kind of biblical interpretation either has had some effect on what used to be called *hermeneutica profana* or offers analogies to the sphere of secular literature. Of course, secular texts have often enough been rejected in the name of religious principle. Both St. Jerome and St. Augustine give every evidence of conflict over their relation to the classical culture which they inherited. Gosson in the sixteenth century attacked the immorality of "profane" poetry and called forth an apologia by Sidney far more enduring than the attack. But such rejections of the secular in the name of the sacred are not based on a method of interpretation. Secular immorality is much too plain and there is no hesitation in discarding it, however prestigious its vehicle. But to attack and subvert the bulk of a sacred, normative work in the name of a small part which is judged to be of transcendent value is an act of interpretation. Marcion, in fact, used a small selection of texts as a hammer with which to destroy the remaining corpus.

The radicalness of Marcion's interpretation of Scripture may be more apparent when we reflect that the Bible, unlike the Homeric poems, was taken to be a historical and not a poetic work. Marcion argues that the God of the Old Testament really exists and that he did the works he is said to have done; only, he is evil. The reader of Homer was not ever pressed to make such a decision. If the religious imagination could reject secular literature as immoral or as a mere fiction, it was also possible to live comfortably with secular literature precisely because it was a fiction. Where it offended moral sensibilities, allegorical interpretation was always at hand. Pagans never had problems of Marcion's kind with their literature and neither did most Christians with the Bible. The problem for Christians lay elsewhere. For centuries, the Christian culture in its secular aspect was thoroughly saturated with allusions and descriptions of the old pagan religion and it was a long time before some

Christians were thoroughly comfortable with their indispensable pagan inheritance. St. Jerome, the patron saint of Christian philologists, tells of having a bad dream in which Christ
reproaches him for being a Ciceronian rather than a Christian,
and a trained Roman lawyer like Tertullian could exclaim in
exasperation and contempt, "What has Athens to do with Jeru-
salem?" Christians, however, managed throughout the Middle
Ages to "save" Virgil or Ovid through elaborate allegorical
interpretations. In the case of Ovid, the demand for allegorical
ingenuity was considerable!

Whatever the rigidities in ancient systems of rhetorical
classification and interpretation, it was always recognized that
literary works had a hypothetical character and that their measure of truth was conveyed in an oblique or "fictional" way.
We may reject allegory but our understanding of literary works
is not far from this. The Bible, unlike *fictiones,* was not only
sacred but historical. If its authors on occasion had recourse to
allegory, parables, figures of speech, and flowers of rhetoric,
the book was nevertheless fundamentally a historical record of
the progress of revelation. To reject the literal meaning of the
book or to judge that meaning as evil was a very different
matter from rejecting the literal meaning of Ovid, Virgil, or
Homer. Subverting a literal biblical meaning meant either denying its essential historicity or, with Marcion, acknowledging
that historicity by making a revolutionary inversion of the value
of the text.

Although modern secular and sceptical temperaments
have long transcended the distinction between the interpretation of a secular text and a sacred text, some distinction between *hermeneutica sacra* and *hermeneutica profana* was conserved in theory until the time of Schleiermacher. Even the
religious man, for Schleiermacher, had to give up this distinction if only because the human mind and the conditions of and
occasions for understanding are really everywhere the same.
We cannot suspend our rational faculties or the methods of
scientific inquiry merely because a text is denominated sacred.
Nor can the believer in the Holy Spirit invoke divine guidance
and rise up from the text with what it "really" means. The
believer may find uses for the sacred text that elude the unbe-

liever, but as the exegete he must follow the same signposts on the road to understanding.

We might observe that this obliteration of theoretical distinction between secular and sacred texts has had two ironic consequences for literary criticism. With Matthew Arnold, religion and its texts enters entirely into the sphere of culture, while the heirs of Coleridge and Jung, those critics whose leading concepts are "symbol" and "archetype," seem to subsume poetry into religious structures.[12]

Thus when Blake thought of poetry as allegory addressed to the intellectual powers, he had in mind the traditions of *allegoria sacra*. But Blake was not concerned to secularize the sacred but to sacralize what others misapprehended as secular, the poetic imagination itself. Certainly he was not concerned to "follow nature" in any sense a classically trained reader would have understood that injunction. To follow nature meant, after all, to follow the secular norms and conventions of classical models. Virgil had imitated nature when he imitated Homer, and Pope had done the same when he imitated Horace.

It is a commonplace to observe that the Romantics broke with neoclassical norms and that in varying ways literature and literary activity had become sacralized in the view of most of them. It has perhaps not been as well noted that with the Romantics the literary influence of the Bible and its traditional exegesis become pronounced in a novel way. Categories of literary construction and literary interpretation of biblical origin are applied to literary activities previously thought of as purely secular. What M. H. Abrams called a "natural supernaturalism" enters the domain of literary interpretation. Poetry and myth become part of a universal revelation flowing from the imagination which, like the author-God of Scripture, states itself in symbol and metaphor. Nature encompasses what once stood opposed to it, and we discern it as abounding in moments of grace if we allow the imagination to penetrate the cloud of habit that stands between us and the world. Philology, in a broad sense of the term, had become a "sacred" discipline, the key to the appropriation of the poetic legacy of the world.

Philology began, of course, as the discipline which aims at the scientific understanding of literary texts, including texts which are not literary in any narrow sense of the word, and it came into being during the Renaissance. The first great triumph of this new science was Lorenzo Valla's demonstration that the *Donation of Constantine* was a forgery. Neither the language of the text nor some of its geographical allusions could be made historically coherent with its presumed date. Nothing quite like this had ever been done before, and even as erudite a man as Dante could only deplore the *Donation* but not dream of questioning its authenticity.

While philology developed largely in the field of classical scholarship, it was soon applied to biblical studies as well. Until Schleiermacher, it was generally understood that although philology made use of hermeneutics, rules of interpretation, at some point in the task of interpretation a distinction would arise in the types of hermeneutics depending on whether the text was secular or sacred. In practice the rules were pretty much the same. As they were formulated by Schleiermacher, at the end of a long tradition, there were several tasks any exegete had to accomplish.

First of all, the exegete had to analyze the manner in which the work was constructed with reference to its characteristic traits of style in order to view the parts in relation to the whole and the whole as encompassing its parts. This principle is little more than what the late Leo Spitzer called the "philological circle," a continual passage from details of style and construction to the whole and back again, a reading and rereading of the work in the light of its details. Applied to Machiavelli's *Prince,* this process might mean taking note of how Machiavelli uses crucial terms like *virtù, fortuna, occasione* to frame the problem of action and how the work as a whole deals with that problem.

A second principle seems obvious but is not perhaps as evident as it seems. The exegete must know the rules of grammar of the language of his text. Since the grammar of Cicero and of St. Jerome, of Plato and of St. Paul, are quite different in important respects, this task was not quite as simple as it sounds.

The exegete also had to be aware of the terminological peculiarities of an author and take special care that he not misinterpret them. Such a problem would arise in misinterpreting the very special ways in which St. Paul uses terms like "soul," "spirit," or "flesh" (*psyche, pneuma,* or *sarx*). It would be easy to attach meanings derived from Platonic authors but quite foreign to the meanings of St. Paul. This task of interpretation leads directly into another, that of ascertaining the cultural environment of the author and determining what sort of terminology may have been current in his time. It is a short step from this to determining the historical circumstances in which a particular work was written. Indeed, grammar, terminology, the cultural and historical circumstances of a work are distinguishable in principle more than in practice. They add up to bringing all possible relevant knowledge to bear on understanding a work.

Beyond these rules lies a further problem, as Schleiermacher and, later, Dilthey both realized. A literary document in particular is expressive of the articulated and interpreted experience of a single, unique individual. What do we mean when we say that we understand this poem, or play, or novel? We might say, with Dilthey, that we are somehow capable of an act of *Verstehen,* of putting ourselves in the author's place and time, even if with difficulty. Our assumption is that language is social and arises from a common human nature, that the common human nature which generates language is what makes *Verstehen* possible. Although languages differ and categorize experience in different ways, translation is always possible, and to understand is something like translation. In one sense, then, language is everywhere the same if only because the brain and nervous system are everywhere the same. This is essentially the thesis of modern structural linguistics. Transformational grammar certainly strips from particular linguistic expression or the special structure of different languages what is individual, indeed "literary," about them, but it does establish a kind of universal grammar which probably has a neurological basis and which is the presupposition of our ability to understand others in speech or in writing and to be conversant with more than one language.[13]

Although understanding presupposes some kind of universalized conception of language and of the nature and function of the brain, it still remains, as Dilthey believed, paradoxically a personal act. Grammatical transformations worked on Shakespeare, for example, would simply remove from his sentences anything of literary value. Indeed, the interpreter of a humanistic text would certainly find the particularistic linguistic emphases of a Whorf or a Sapir more germane to his task: as languages shape reality in different ways, so the poet uses the resources of language to further differentiate those shapings. A poet is, foremost, a linguistic innovator in a particular language, although he works within the categories of understanding that apply to all languages.

The foregoing account of classic theories of interpretation assumes that the task of the interpreter is to ascertain authorial intention. When we understand, we understand what someone wants us to understand. All the rules and their application serve simply to permit this act of understanding to happen. In a way, the classic theory of interpretation was "psychological" in that it posited two minds, the author's and the reader's, which somehow met through the mediation of language.[14]

With Heidegger another exegetical possibility was disclosed. A text may reveal *indirectly* a "life-feeling" or a particular understanding of existence, and this may be true of very unliterary or unexpressive texts like codes of law or chronologies written in Egyptian hieroglyphics. Clearly the person who discerns a particular attitude toward existence in a text brings to it a question which the text was not written to answer. Thus, a historical document may be read for the light it gives to events, but it may also be read to discern how the historian viewed those events, an intention which may not have been present to his conscious mind. Whether such an understanding of a text should be referred to as its "meaning" or as its "significance" is an important question, and it does confuse matters to refer to such indirect disclosures as *the meaning* of a text.[15]

Certainly, the questions we bring to a text may differ profoundly, and what we understand will differ accordingly. The scholar interested in the historical reconstruction of an era will often enough read a text for clues concerning events or social practices which have entered the document inadvertently. Or, according to Schleiermacher and Dilthey, he will finally understand the text in much the same way one might understand an interlocuter, in some "psychological" sense. So-called formalist critics subject a poem to "aesthetic" analysis and are less interested in what the text says in some crudely direct way than what it says after they discern and understand the peculiarities of style, ambiguities of meaning, and rhythmical nuances of language. Existential interpretation would appear to differ from these in asking of a text what possibilities it may disclose of human existence.

Religious, philosophical, and poetic texts more than any other kinds do in fact present us with statements of self-understanding. We can always ask of a Shakespeare play: what is life in this play taken to be like? Having asked such a question of *King Lear*—at least after having read Heidegger—we can in fact emerge with a reading of the play that gives it a contemporaneousness the literary scholar might find too far removed from the texture of the play itself. The play is more than the disclosure of an attitude toward existence. Nevertheless, we may read such humanistic texts with our historical imagination alert to grasping in events, real and imaginary, the various particular potentialities of human existence. The text may claim no more than that it is a poem, or a play, or a religious revelation, or a philosophical dialogue, but we are not confined by that claim.

Rudolf Bultmann is, in exegetical matters, Heidegger's best known follower and finds in the philosopher's *Being and Time* a decisive advance in the theory of interpretation. In this work Heidegger advances the thesis of "preunderstanding," the idea that the kind of question the exegete brings to the text is an essential component of the act of understanding it. This is by no means an arbitrary act in which the exegete simply finds what he wants to find; nor does the exegete with specific questions prejudice the outcome of his inquiry.[16] What is brought to the text as preunderstanding is a "life-relationship" to the subject matter, something other than the common human nature in Schleiermacher's sense. Scientific understanding is, in this view, independent of the person of the scientist, while historical understanding is open to the interpreter only as the text he reads is bound up with his own history. A text must be understood "subjectively," or existentially, if it is to be understood "authentically."

The concept of preunderstanding in Heidegger and Bultmann rests on an analysis of the hermeneutical circle. All understanding presupposes preunderstanding; the answer is in a way determined by the question. The answer also corrects the question. Preunderstanding is continually modified by new answers and so generates new understanding. True understanding, existential or authentic understanding, is always new understanding. It continually involves "decision," not in the sense of an act of the will, but in the sense in which understanding of a humanistic-historical text involves what we must call acts of self-recognition. Since the self is, from this point of view, a historical continuum, the hermeneutical circle is not to be avoided. As Heidegger puts it "What is decisive is not to get out of the circle but to come into it in the right way."[17]

The circle appears in more than one manifestation. The critic who studies a poem by continually and repetitively proceeding from part to whole and back again is involved in the hermeneutical circle, which Spitzer preferred to call the philological circle. The scholar who determines the authorship of a text on the basis of the author's terminology, although the terminology is defined by the whole context of the text itself, is also involved in this kind of 'virtuous" and not vicious circularity. A similar pattern discloses itself when the interpreter studies the text in the light of its historical and cultural background, or when he attempts to determine the purpose of a difficult text by repeatedly examining parts in relation to what gradually reveals itself as the intention of the whole.

The esoteric terminology of Heideggerian philosophy may hide the fact, as one astute critic of Bultmann and Heidegger observed, that preunderstanding rests on our capacity to understand the genre. We recognize by the character of the work's statements what category it falls into. If we have read enough poems, histories, or novels, we are not especially puzzled by the fact that a novelist can read the minds of his characters, or that poetic metaphors might frequently be absurd if taken literally, or that historians draw conclusions about events they have never witnessed and even write as if they had participated in events that occurred long before they were born.[18]

A particular system of conventions is perhaps as good an equivalent for "genre" in this context as any. The whole of our intellectual training teaches us, as it must, how to recognize genre. We laugh at a parody of a poem or play precisely because the conventions may be used in a context that is inappropriate to them. Convention, as Northrop Frye expressed it, constitutes a kind of "contract" between the author and the reader about how the author is permitted to say what he wants to say. "Once upon a time," although it is rarely true that what follows happened, is a convention which introduces what we know to be a fairy tale. To go along with the author is much like going along with a scientific hypothesis. In each case we are asked to make an assumption, more or less gratuitously, in the interest of seeing what may follow.

When a reader cannot accept the conventions of a particular genre, a work simply becomes unintelligible. Dr. Johnson's attack on Milton's *Lycidas* because it mixed the sacred and the profane, and because shepherds are not like Milton portrays them, is one good example of the failure of preunderstanding in this contractual sense. Johnson simply refused to contract with his author.

Of course, Heideggerian exegesis seeks to go beyond such mundane formulations and poses the question of "authentic" questioning of a text. This means—and I must here use the terminology of the school—seeking in a text answers to questions concerning the "possibilities of existence." This does not simply mean access to another set of values, or another view of the world. Authentic questioning of a text presupposes that the exegete's existence is not assured, is "not at his own disposal." Authentic questioning is not an "objective" enterprise, nor does the exegete preserve his distance from the text. Only if he understands, as all men apparently should, that existence is problematical, that it is not under man's control, does he approach a text ready to acknowledge it as making claims on him to "decide." Here again, I take "decision" to mean self-recognition, the act of finding in a text a decisive interpretation of human experience and the human condition.

Clearly the paradigm for this kind of reading is the Bible, although neither Heidegger nor his theological disciples would deny the possibility of reading other texts in this way. Indeed, all "historical" texts should be read "authentically." Certainly, "authentic" readings, like any others, are various. When we consider the vast bulk of commentary and interpretation that has been generated by the classics, or Shakespeare, not to mention the Bible, we can only conclude with Heidegger that the hermeneutical circle of understanding is indeed endless. It is also clear that, however "authentic" the reading of a text, only a particular aspect of it is given to a reader to understand at his specific place and time. The "significance," the "applicability," the "authenticity" of an interpretation is endlessly variable, and it neither can nor should be otherwise.

But at this point one might object that it is only in the light of some conception of the determinative importance of authorial intention that we can ever claim to limit interpretative variability to what is not arbitrary or trivial. The very point which existentialist interpretation finds so difficult to accept or treats as indeterminable, is the only principle we have which permits us to judge some interpretations as negating criteria of historical understanding. But Heidegger is not really concerned with the historical reading of poetic and philosophical texts, not, at any rate, of those texts which are instances of "primary" rather than "secondary" thinking. Insofar as language discloses "being," the specifications of existence and its possibilities, authorial intention is no more important than it would be to a pious reader of the Psalms.

The instances of interpretative activities I have discussed in this chapter disclose that the peculiar problems of biblical interpretation have had compelling consequences for the history of interpretation in general. Although largely conservative in tendency, biblical exegesis found a subverter in Marcion, at least, and there have since been others less religiously inspired. But the secularization of *hermeneutica sacra* and its amalgamation to *hermeneutica profana* open the way to two opposing tendencies in modern humanistic and literary interpretation: the sacralization of the secular and the secularization of the sacred. Heidegger is surely the heir of many of the Romantics in vastly extending the corpus of revelatory texts to include poetry, and a critic like Leavis is not far from basing a complete moral education on literary texts. It would not be impossible to set most of our leading interpreters—a Coleridge, an Arnold, a Jaspers—on one or another side of this polarity.

Style as Interpretation

IF WE GIVE TO the idea of interpretation its widest possible latitude, then every text we interpret is itself—in style, in symbolic and metaphorical texture—an interpretation, a "revelation." Whatever the shortcomings of Heideggerian theories of interpretation, they grasp this truth very clearly. But the concept is older than Heidegger. The status of every text as an expression and interpretation of reality is well developed in Vico's *Scienza Nova*. Where Heidegger would say that the text interprets "being," or realizes "being," Vico might say that the text is a *factum,* something made by the mind of man, therefore intelligible to man and so a modality of truth, for *factum et verum convertuntur*. When one says that a text in and of itself is an interpretation of reality, the obscure word, of course, is "reality." In Vico's context, reality does not mean something "out there" in the world of nature. Vico thought that nature, as God's *factum,* was not *essentially* knowable. True, we have a good deal of knowledge of the natural world and will doubtless have more, but the concepts of science are constructs by which we deal with a world whose full complexity eludes us. Indeed, the concepts of science simplify and abstract from the richness of experience, and must lose that richness in order to render aspects of the world intelligible and capable of manipulation. Confronted with modern technology, Vico might have altered his views somewhat. Machines may be viewed as *facta* and Vico might have had interesting things to say about mechanical models of natural functioning. But his understanding of science was shaped by the dominance of the Cartesian tradition with its emphasis on mathematics and on a hypothetic-deductive methodology.

In any event, reality is not for Vico a fixed truth which each thinker gets a bit closer to, but something of which each thinker gives us his own perspective. It is an "object" identical with understanding and articulation, and appears only with understanding and articulation. There is no other way in which we possess any reality at all. It is not a constant which successive writers or thinkers imitate or represent. The sum of the literature and thought of the world does not add up to the description of a reality "external" to us. It is something we struggle with language to apprehend and does not, in this sense, preexist that struggle. The effect of a Chaucer or Shakespeare on the English language, for example, is to give us a language with which more "reality" is placed at our disposal. So Vico might have argued that consciousness does evolve through great writers.

Of course, the term "reality" in this context does not mean what it does in current literary criticism, where it often refers to social reality of a particular time and place, or to "everyday" life of one kind or another. Neither does it have another meaning, also current, in which "reality" is disclosed in a tragic or catastrophic crisis that disrupts the even flow of everyday reality.[1] Vico's concept of reality is more inclusive and would comprehend these meanings as dialectical polarities which imply each other as surely as subject and object.

The world of everyday reality is, often enough, penetrated by a glimpse of other realities from which the world shields us but which it also defines by contrast. Erich Kahler, in fact, proposed that the history of any "reality" is in substance the history of consciousness, a history which has left its record in the long evolution of narrative.[2]

According to this thesis we can discern in the record of narrative a struggle of consciousness to define and locate reality. The earliest writings which tend toward a rational view of events are chronicles. They express a reality conceived entirely in terms of what Kahler calls "outer space." Events are totally objectified, if I understand Kahler correctly. They are also simply recorded in a temporal sequence; I would therefore add the notion of "outer" or "linear" time to Kahler's analysis at this point.

The progress of consciousness is signalled by the appearance of narrative proper, which replaces chronicle and in which we find the first representation of "inner space." Inner space is that mode of perceiving and rendering events which discloses human beings as agents of action, endowed with motive and subjectivity. In this respect, the Bible and the Homeric poems are our earliest true narratives.

Auerbach, in contrast to Kahler, discerned a profound difference between the meaning of human life as portrayed in the Bible and in the *Odyssey*. Biblical narrative depends on its background for full significance. Events are continually played out in relation to a supreme divine activity and in a world in which this divine agency may define an ultimate significance other than that immediately evident in the actions of men, however motivated from within. The *Odyssey* is articulated in terms of its foreground. The sequences of events are highly modulated, details abound and may be charged with the highest significance. There is no background in the biblical sense, for the Homeric gods are really humans with special powers. True, they are immortal and generally are free from sufferings, but, except for their immortality, there is no truly radical difference between them and the humans they observe. Over human and divine reality rests fate, and a single cosmos contains both gods and men. Auerbach brings these contrasts and others to a single focus in his juxtaposition of two episodes, Abraham's sacrifice of Isaac in Genesis and the recognition of Odysseus' scar by his old nurse, the most critical of the many recognition scenes which appear in the epic.

In the former, reality comes to birth in a crisis of excruciating intensity. God apparently contradicts his own moral nature, and trust in God is put to its severest test. Ultimate crisis reveals a truth about both God and Abraham. The narrative of the Bible, and the one appropriate to the reality discerned and interpreted in this story, is paratactic, sentences juxtaposed and coordinated with no subordination and no need for subordination. God commands, man acts, obeys, and discloses himself. The recognition narrative of Odysseus' scar, on the other hand, reveals a highly differentiated and modulated reality, the gradual disclosure of an identity through a singular clue, the

suppression of the revelation of that identity, and its ultimate
disclosure through subsequent acts of recognition. The style of
Homer is and must be hypotactic, units of meaning requiring
subordination if the narrative is to unfold. Where Auerbach
drew a contrast of the highest significance, Kahler discerns a
unity, in that both biblical and Homeric narrative disclose men
as agents of decision and action.

For Kahler, the advent of Christianity creates a new kind
of narrative, narrative with "imposed meaning." The agents of
action are all participants in what is essentially a transcendental
drama and acquire their significance from an incessant divine
activity which relates mundane events and realities to a transcendental sphere. I am not at all sure that Christianity can be
considered as the sole initiator of this kind of narrative. Surely,
something like this is implicit in the frequent divine intrusions
and judgments of the Old Testament narrative. It is nevertheless true that Christianity greatly heightened this tendency; a
work like St. John's Gospel is structurally arranged around the
analogous but contrasting relations between this world and a
totally different one. The kingdom of this world and that other
kingdom are to each other as dark and light, as truth and lie,
because the Fall has intervened to distort the original fair copy
and turn it into a divine ruin.

For Kahler, individual psychology first appears in the Renaissance with the narratives of Petrarch and Boccaccio, who
enrich the inner space of narrative with the description of psychological processes and states, an innovation which, in increasing measure, marks all of the subsequent development of
narrative. It has long been recognized that the stories of Boccaccio are often enough secularized versions of moral exemplary tales, or even of hagiographical lives. We would have to
say, if we pursue Kahler's line of thought, that such narratives
derive from secularized or even parodistic adaptations of the
"imposed" meaning in the Christian narratives.

Lest we assume that the history of narrative is nothing
more than the progression of subjectivity, Kahler takes account
of the appearance of social realities in narrative. Thus, the
growth of urban life during the Middle Ages, with its contrasts
between the man-made city and the God-made landscape and

between the city-dweller and the courtly aristocracy, creates the "romantic situation." It is surely true, as Kahler emphasizes, that these social contrasts which developed with the progressive urbanization of Europe in the Middle Ages and with the increase of wealth and commerce did set up a situation in which the country and court could provide an ideal realm of the imagination for those who did not inhabit either. But such a situation had in fact occurred elsewhere and much earlier in the history of literature. The ideal pastoral landscape of Theocritus, Longus, and Virgil was surely the result of a very similar "romantic situation." One has to have great cosmopolitan cities like Alexandria and Rome before he can yearn for Arcadia. But it is important to bear in mind that neither medieval nor ancient literature deal with social realities for their own sake. We may, of course, infer from classical pastoral or courtly romance what sort of social attitudes obtained in some quarters at some times, but only in satire and in some lyrics can we find a more direct presentation of and judgment on social reality. A comprehensive social realm as the subject of literature is a distinctively modern phenomenon.

The appearance of the "romantic situation" not withstanding, narrative in the Middle Ages remained within the Christian cosmology, in that events, as in Dante, take their significance from a higher reality, in what Kahler calls a system of "descending symbolism." Only with the great narrative of Cervantes does an "ascending symbolism" appear for the first time. Cervantes proceeds from the delineation of an individual, but one whose significance gradually expands to encompass a universal meaning. This larger meaning transcends the individual, but is without reference to a transcendental realm of being and value. According to Kahler, such an ascending symbolism is foreign not only to Christianity but to Greek literature as well.

Kahler's thesis is probably too schematic and a little too reminiscent of the inexorable march of Hegel's absolute spirit through history. Nevertheless, his view does call attention to the various ways in which style is interpretation and to the special relation man has to his own culture, as an object of understanding, in distinction to the relation he has to the natural world. Perhaps it is not as much the ghost of Hegel who hovers over Kahler's book as the ghost of Vico.

Kahler would probably have agreed with the Italian philosopher that, in some special sense, man can truly know only what he makes, the records and artifacts of his activity over time. The "inexactitude" of such knowledge and the variations in understanding the records and artifacts of civilization are irrelevant to the truth of this proposition. Both the nature of man *qua* man and his knowledge of that nature are historical, changing with time, yet recognizable and knowable despite change. The history of human consciousness is simply the history of what man creates, that cultural, social, historical world which constitutes the intimate environment interposed between himself and his natural environment. Obviously, man stands in a different relationship to nature than to culture. The world of nature is God's world, "il mondo della natura," while man's world is "il mondo delle nazioni." To the extent that Vico draws a radical distinction between nature and culture, we need not and should not entirely agree with him. Nor need we agree that true knowledge is possible only of culture, while knowledge of nature is merely relative.

In fact, Vico did not take these distinctions as far as did some of his German admirers, and his distinction between scientific knowledge and historical knowledge is by no means simplistic. He grasped that the difficulties of historical understanding emerged from the variousness and richness of human life, while the presumed exactitudes of science arose by abstracting from the richness and variety of nature and imposing simplified but workable constructs upon it. However strange the evidences of history may be, the historian knows that they are nevertheless evidence of what man has been. He might have to conclude that man is more strange than he thought. The scientist, in a sense, ignores what used to be called the secondary qualities of experience, all the color, smells, buzz and confusion, to grasp those relations which can be discerned and, preferably, measured.

Vico's essential question is how knowledge of the past is possible, given the mutability of all things human and the inevitability of cultural and historical change. Vico answers by positing a *sensus communis generis humani,* a faculty of understanding which does not change, although man does. It is simply the faculty that makes the records and creations of the past intelligible. True, such a notion is really an affirmation and not the demonstration of anthing in particular. But in this Vico is no different from his successors Schleiermacher or Dilthey, who also argue that we understand past documents because they were made by men like ourselves with whom we share a common nature. Although it is obvious that all things change and that large regions of the past may at first appear remote, whatever man has done can be understood with the exercise of reason, learning, and imagination.

This common tie with all other men living and dead is finally identifiable as language, and so that discipline of understanding the past was essentially philology. But philology in that broad sense in which, if a scholar really wanted to understand the Latin word *lex* or *ius,* he read the corpus of Roman law. This kind of philology was the key, as Michelet put it, to the "résurrection de la vie intégrale" (i.e., of the past).

The most remarkable modern contribution to elucidating the manner in which literature interprets reality is certainly that of Erich Auerbach, a self-proclaimed disciple of Vico.[3] In his book *Dante als Dichter der Irdischen Welt,* Auerbach gave us a fresh interpretation of the *Divine Comedy* as a poem which encompasses all of the complexity, variety, and conflict of human experience—as any great poem must—but locates experience in a transcendental realm which confers a final ethical ordering.

> Thus, in truth the *Divine Comedy* is a picture of earthly life. The human world in all its breadth and depth is gathered into the structure of the hereafter and there it stands: complete, unfalsified, yet encompassed in an ethical order; the confusion of earthly affairs is not concealed or attenuated or immaterialized, but preserved in full evidence and grounded in a plan which embraces it and raises it above all contingency.[4]

Auerbach's view of Dante draws upon the insights of two great German philosophers of Romanticism, Schelling and Hegel. Schelling, in his essay "Dante in philosophischer Bezie-

hung,'' had described the *Divine Comedy* as a poem prophetic
of the modern age, as the first paradigm of a modern poem.
Schelling was quite self-consciously aware of participating in a
new cultural movement, which we have come to call Romanticism, in which a great achievement was ''the discovery of the
Individual.'' Dante's poem then is ''modern'' because the
poet's focus of awareness is on particulars and individuals, not
on generalities. In Dante's poem we first find the singular,
unique individual, in possession of a kind of ultimate significance formerly conferred on the individual only as the em-
bodiment of a class, a species, or genus. Every character in the
Divine Comedy comes to us through a style expressing individual history and destiny. At the same time as each character is
unique and comes to a unique end, we are asked, according to
Schelling, to view the same character allegorically, in terms of
a finally defined ethical state through which the individual
achieves eternal significance.[5] The final place of each individual
in Dante's scheme is a place defined as having general and
universal meaning. But each singular character brings himself
to that place and thus defines it as well as is defined by it.

Schelling saw Dante as the precursor of the modern age, at
least as a Romantic might define modernity. But if Harnack
was correct in claiming that Christianity contributed to the religious history of mankind the concept of the infinite worth of the
individual, then Dante may just as well be viewed as the first
poet to realize this Christian view of human reality. After all,
even eternal damnation is but the negative of infinite worth.
Why else would the Almighty require an eternity of torment?
We might, looking back on Schelling, see this particular Romantic view of individuality and modernity as a secularization
of the Christian concept which Dante still conserved within the
sphere of the sacred.

Hegel, in his *Ästhetik,* had offered a similar view of
Dante's achievement.

> Here all individuality, every singularity of human interest
> and purpose disappear before the absolute magnitude of
> the ultimate end and goal of all things; at the same time,
> however, the transitoriness and fleetingness of the living
> world, viewed objectively in its innermost workings and,

in all its dignity and wretchedness dependent upon God's Providence, are depicted in fullness and variety. For just as individuals were in this life, in their passions and sufferings, their ambitions and achievements, so are they now shown here forever, in the life beyond, hardened and immobilized like bronze figures. In this respect, the poem encompasses the totality of life: the eternal state of Hell, Purgatory, and Paradise, and upon this indestructible foundation persons from our everyday world move in accordance with their particular temperament and character; or rather, they HAVE moved and are now, in their being and actions, finally, eternally, and aesthetically fixed.[6]

Schelling, Hegel, and Auerbach all discerned in Dante the rendering of the individual as identical with his unique history and fate, the person as the sum of all his acts of decision, defined in a final state of universal significance by the will as it reached that state through all of its choices from moment to moment in the course of its temporal existence. This singular historicity of the individual, although unique, defines him in terms of a system of universal moral value and thus permits us to see in ordinary life qualities of universal or tragic significance. It is true that Dante picks the inhabitants of the other world from those more or less known to fame, but they come from all walks of life and are representative of the whole of humanity. Here if anywhere we find Hegel's concrete universal, the synthesis of individuality and universality. From this point of view, Montaigne is the true heir of Dante, for in his work we find ordinary and everyday experience opening out into the tragic, the comic, and the universal.

This possibility of interpreting reality was, according to Auerbach, determined by two great and important revolutions in ''sensibility'' brought about by Christianity. The one is the figural or typological view of history, and the other is the impact of the Bible, the New Testament in particular, in breaking down classical genre theory.

The tradition of Graeco-Roman rhetorical theory as finally codified and transmitted to Western Europe by Cicero, Quintillian, and Pliny had formulated a rigorous correlation between levels of style and subject matter. Tradition had established three levels of style, applied as well to the spoken and the written word and strictly correlated to what might be called the "level" of the subject to be written or spoken about. All subjects of tragic import or high seriousness were to achieve expression in the high style, the *sermo gravis* or *sermo sublimis*. The *sermo temperatus,* or the "mediocre style," was appropriate for a somewhat odd group of subjects: persuasion and dissuasion, social satire, eulogistic or encomiastic works. The low style, or *sermo humilis,* was confined to the least elevated subjects: everyday life as lived by ordinary people, relatively unimportant matters, comic situations and characters, anything crudely erotic or scatological.

This genre theory has influenced literary ideals and practice virtually down to our own time. Obviously, the Romantics rejected it, but as long as a classical education was the norm for the Western intelligentsia, it continued to exert its influence. At times, in French or even English neo-classicism, it flourished, at least in principle, with extraordinary vigor. With the written records of the story of Christ and the entry of the Bible into Western civilization as the central book, genre theory was challenged wherever Christian intellectuals looked to scriptural inspiration and scriptural models. Although St. Augustine never ceased to write like a classically trained Roman rhetorician, in *De Doctrina Christiana* he defended a style faithful to truth, however lacking in *eloquentia,* against the doctrines of the rhetorical schools. Scripture might not obey the rules of rhetoric and style as contemporary pagan intellectuals understood them, but its truth possessed a beauty below the level of style and mere verbal dexterity.

In the story of Christ, his journey as a preacher, his betrayal, and his sufferings, in the vision of Christ as the incarnation in a humble man of the Divinity Himself, the correlation of style and subject matter is shattered. The death on the cross was the death of a criminal, but this death is the redemptive act for all mankind. The great story not only unites the sublime with the humble in subject matter; it is written in a language, *koine* Greek, which was not the language of the trained literary intellectual of the period, but the *lingua franca* of the hellenized East. To the extent that this story dominated a writer's imagination, he was open to ignoring the correlation of style and subject matter. Hence, medieval literature often enough falls out of the classical pattern. After Curtius' *European Literature and the Latin Middle Ages,* few students of literature have any excuse for not realizing the pervasive influence of classical antiquity on the Middle Ages, but Auerbach's thesis is in its essentials correct. The *Divine Comedy* is not a classical work, however much, intellectually and aesthetically, Dante was drawn to the Roman world.

Auerbach does not attend closely to other factors which served to break genre theory in the Middle Ages. He has little to say of the introduction of traditions which were neither Christian nor classical. I refer in particular to the Germanic and Celtic mythology which had its own powerful effect on medieval romance and chronicle.

Nevertheless, his thesis on the effect of the Bible and of *Imitatio Christi* is determinative. For in the story of the Incarnation, Crucifixion, and Resurrection, the themes of exaltation and humiliation, *sublimitas* and *humilitas,* combine to create the most astounding paradox of our whole cultural tradition. St. Paul grasped this when he recognized that the Greeks seek after wisdom, the Jews seek a "sign," the eschatological Messiah who will restore Israel, but Christianity preaches Christ crucified—"unto the Greeks foolishness and unto the Jews a stumbling-block."

> The story of Christ . . . transcended the limits of ancient mimetic aesthetics. . . . The classical division of genres has vanished; the distinction between the lofty and the vulgar style no longer exists . . . in the Gospels, as in ancient comedy, real persons of all classes make their appearance: fishermen and kings, high priests, publicans, and harlots participate in the action; and neither do those of exalted rank act in the style of classical tragedy nor do the lowly behave as in a farce; on the contrary, all social and aesthetic limits have been effaced. . . . The depth and scope of the naturalism in the story of Christ are unparalleled; neither the poets nor the historians of antiquity had the opportunity or the power to narrate human events in that way.[7]

The Christian vision opened the imagination to a new relation between the Supreme Reality and everyday reality, so that
no social class or occupation or condition in life was without that
eternal reference, whether for good or evil. Christianity created
a view of the significance of the human actors on the stage of
history which also conferred abiding significance on events of
the temporal process and the agents of historical action.

Of course, Jewish thought had evolved a prophetic interpretation of history. We find evidence in eschatological and
apocalyptic writings of the return of a great historical figure
such as Elijah as the herald of a new age, or the coming of a
messianic deliverer who is the fulfillment of a typological precursor. Figural or typological interpretation in its highly developed form, however, is the result of the attempt to read Christian revelation as everywhere predicted in the Old Testament.
The historical record of God's dealings with Israel is a record
of God's preparation for the Incarnation if we read it right.

This conception of typological prophecy is already present
in the Pauline literature, both in the epistles indubitably his and
very markedly in the epistle to the Hebrews, certainly not from
the hand of Paul. This method of interpretation quite simply
established some kind of relation between two figures and
events separated in time. The first is taken to signify in a shadowy way as *umbra* or *figura* what the second term of the analogy expresses clearly as *imago*. The first term is a real person
or event—the Flood, Moses, or any other such reality—but it is
also a sign or figure of the second, prophesying it and pointing
to the second as its fulfillment. Moses, for example, is a type of
Christ; among the many clues we are offered to this analogy is
the forty days on Horeb-Sinai of the one and the forty days in
the wilderness of the other.

From the prophetic point of view, all kinds of typological
analogies suggest themselves. Adam is a type or antitype of
Christ, the first man bringing death and sin into the world, the
second man bringing light and truth. The Flood is a type or
antitype of Baptism; the contrast here is drawn between the
waters which are the punishment of sin and the waters which
wash it away and save the individual. The Ark which saves the
remnant of life is also a type of Christ, for he rescues us from

the universal deluge of sin and death. If Adam stands in contrast to Christ in a kind of antithesis, Moses prefigures him positively. The Exodus which Moses led is a type of that spiritual exodus, in which Christ is our leader, out of the Egypt of sin into the Canaan of salvation.[8]

The type and the fulfillment of type or antitype are related not only to each other but to a transcendental or eschatological reality. It is true that the Old Testament everywhere prophesies Christ, but it is also true that the New Testament points to the eschatological end-time which will bring complete fulfillment with the end of history.

Obviously, the historiography implicit in this view of events is quite different either from cyclical theories of history, such as we might find in Polybius or Vico, or from the progressivistic view of history which has dominated modern thought. We view events as moving in a more or less linear pattern towards an endless future, regardless of our guesses as to what that future might bring. Figural or typological history, on the other hand, views the historical sequence as bifurcated in terms of a prophetic period and a second period fulfilling the prophecy; the latter period in turn points to the end of history whose essential meaning has now been revealed. Prophetic events and fulfilled events mean each other. This is far from a simple notion of recurrence, both because the fulfillment is more than its prophetic forerunner and because revelation has given us the essential outlines of the transcendental pattern and meaning of all temporal events.

Auerbach also analyzed the literary consequences of the Christian revaluation of suffering, or *passio*. In the Aristotelian tradition, *passio* was correlated with *actio* and was simply the capacity to be acted upon, familiar to us also as the Aristotelian correlates of *potentia* and *actus,* or *dynamis* and *energeia.* The Stoics transferred the concept of *passio* to the moral and psychological sphere. The plural, *passiones,* described those emotions and desires which disturbed the tranquility, or *apatheia,* of the sage. Thus the correlate of *passio* in the Stoic system is not *actio* but *ratio,* reason as the hegemonic principle whose task is to order the perturbations of the soul. Senecan tragedy perhaps fails as drama simply because each tragedy is meant solely to illustrate the dreadful consequences of a single all-dominating passion, jealousy in *Medea,* revenge in *Atreus,* and so on.

In Christianity, suffering must be revalued. The mystery of the suffering servant of Deutero-Isaiah blossoms fully in the Christian story. Through the suffering of the wholly innocent man, a redemption is achieved for guilty man. The Christian, therefore, must accept suffering and must conquer the world and himself through this acceptance of suffering. Although the Stoic and the Christian would have agreed on the necessity of eliminating many worldly desires, the Stoic would not have accepted any form of pain as somehow redemptive. Indeed, it could only be an evil, since it would disturb that tranquility and rationality which is the supreme good.

Although Christian ethics incorporated a good deal of Stoicism into its code of behavior—beginning with the lists of duties, the so-called *Haustafeln* of the later epistles of the New Testament—Christian and Stoic had to part company on the supreme redemptive value of a certain kind of suffering. Although the sacred story everywhere expresses the conception of suffering as a supreme value, it was a long time before the secularization of this value gave to the passions a positively heroic quality. The drama of Racine first gives to feeling, even painful feeling, a positive valuation which has no complete precedent. I would include Shakespeare, however, as giving us such a view of passion along with the Senecan view of passion as a conflict with reason. Certainly, *Antony and Cleopatra* cannot be subsumed satisfactorily into the passion-reason scheme of conflict that some scholars have taken to be the mainspring of Shakespearian tragedy.[9]

In sum, Auerbach proposed that Christianity had transformed style, the interpretation of reality, in three ways:

First, it shattered the tripartite theory of style levels normative in classical rhetorical and literary theory. Certainly, this effect of Christian influence points to a decisive turn of cultural events. I have already suggested that the great influence on medieval vernacular literature of Celtic and Germanic myths and legends exerted a similar influence, of which Auerbach takes little account. He would perhaps have argued that the literature of Arthurian Romance had already been subjected to the Christian influence, in his definition of that influence, but there is surely some importance to the fact that a literary modality neither classical nor Christian was present to the authors of these works. To what degree and in what way such influence also served to break the classical norms which many of the same authors also knew is a matter of scholarly conjecture.

Second, Christianity introduced a kind of historical perspectivism which related events and persons to an eternal meaning via analogies, correspondences, and similitudes. It is this conception of reality which is the presupposition for the "eternalization" of everyday events and individuals in all their particularity.

Third, Christianity reversed the meaning of suffering in the Stoic morality and thereby inaugurated a process which ultimately gave to the feelings and passions a positive meaning in secular terms.

Taken all together, these transformations add up to what Auerbach called Christian realism, the conviction of the permanence and eternal significance of the individual and the appearance of individuals from all classes and conditions as actors in the single historical drama of salvation. These changes served to make the Bible a single book even if it is really a collection of books. What one modern critic, Northrop Frye, requires of biblical criticism has long obtained.

> A genuine higher criticism of the Bible, therefore, would be a synthesizing process which would start with the assumption that the Bible is a definitive myth, a single archetypal structure extending from creation to apocalypse. Its heuristic principle would be St. Augustine's axiom that the Old Testament is revealed in the New and the New concealed in the Old: that the two testaments are not so much allegories of one another as metaphorical identifications of one another. We cannot trace the Bible back, even historically, to a time when its materials were not being shaped into a typological unity, and if the Bible is to be regarded as inspired in any sense, sacred or secular, its editorial and redacting processes must be regarded as inspired too.[10]

An approach to style as content and interpretation, much like that of Auerbach, has been fruitful in modern biblical theological scholarship. Indeed, a good deal of modern biblical theology must strike laymen, at least, as identical with literary criticism, even if theological conclusions are drawn from such analyses. The Christian paradoxes, for example, are seen to govern the style and structure of St. John's gospel. Antithetical concepts are everywhere in the discourses of this book: light and darkness, truth and falsehood, this-world and other-world reality, freedom and bondage, life and death, what is "above" and what is "below." All of these contrasts are rooted in the ultimate contrast between the true world of God and the false world of sinful man. The conversations of Jesus with the people he encounters, Nicodemus or the Samaritan woman at the well, often turn on misunderstandings concerning two distinct realms of being and value. Man in sin mistakes the meaning of rebirth, confounds ordinary water with the water of life, ordinary bread with the bread of life, the true vine with the false. This dualism is not really a metaphysical one, but a dualism of value, will, and power. Men are really blind although they think they see. This blindness leads them to invert paradoxically the true significance of life, mistake their true nature and destiny, and mistake what is a false good for a true one.

Similarly, a dominant peculiarity of Pauline style, the juxtaposition of indicative and imperative, reveals itself as the key to St. Paul's conception of the Christian situation. The indicative, e.g., "you are redeemed," or "you are free from sin," assures the Christian of the reality of his salvation. Its juxtaposition to the imperative, e.g., "now sin no more," tells the Christian that his salvation is not something he simply has, but something he assumes at each moment of his existence. St. Paul says (1 Cor: 5) "Cleanse out the old leaven that you may be as fresh dough, as you really are unleavened."[11]

This peculiar and insistent stylistic construction is an expression of the dialectic of faith. Indicative and imperative imply each other. Faith appropriates salvation as an indicative, but realizes itself as an imperative, as the power to act the command to achieve a new life through faith. St. Paul thus subsumes the imperative of the law into a scheme which transcends the law as simply an imperative. If faith transcends the law, it also makes the substance of the law possible. The imperative thus becomes a call to realize one's salvation, a summons to faith, a summons to continue in the salvation one has appropriated through faith.

Modern interest in the manner that style and language interpret reality has been greatly if indirectly affected by a general theory of the arts that we call by the rather unfortunate name "aesthetics." I say unfortunate because it seems to set the arts off from mental activities aimed at truth and to unify activities which do not easily lend themselves to unification. For the history of interpretation, the most important work dealing with the possibilities and limitations of any particular artistic medium is still Lessing's *Laocoön* (1766). In that work on the limits of poetry and painting, Lessing argues that certain kinds of subject matter are appropriate to plastic or "space" arts and others to literature, a "time" art. (Music, although a "time" art par excellence, cannot easily be understood as possessing a subject, at least in the sense that poems or paintings can possess a subject, so Lessing had to confine his discussion to sculpture and poetry.)

His argument starts with a comparison between the statue of Laocoön, discovered in Rome in 1506, which portrays the Trojan priest of Apollo and his two sons entwined and knotted by two serpentine sea monsters, and a passage describing the same event in Book II of the *Aeneid*.[12]

Lessing maintains that the poet is capable of portraying the suffering of the victims while the sculptor must suppress that very suffering in the interest of the plastic values essential to a space art. Virgil conveys the dynamics of the struggle, with all its terror and pain, more expressively and with greater animation than the sculptor. The statue must, in the nature of things, be formally balanced, composed, so the struggle *qua* struggle is best conveyed by the poet. But the sculptor was right for his task. He expresses the grandeur of the struggle, its monumental quality, a quality which can be grasped *totum simul* in an instant of time through representation in space. The poet, free to move through time, can convey those qualities of the imaginary event which are only displayed serially in time.

Each artist obeys the inherent possibilities and limitations of his medium.

Lessing's brilliant analysis still has great value for us, although it does not reckon with modern attempts to render one art in terms suggestive of another. I do not refer here to the Baroque devices of painting a wall to look sculptured, or other analogous metaphorical "deceptions" in poetry. I have in mind the kind of literary works written by a Virginia Woolf, a Proust, or a Joyce, works which suggest formal qualities of a quasi-spatial character. Neither *Ulysses,* nor *Finnegans Wake,* nor *Swann's Way,* nor *Mrs. Dalloway* pursues the ideal of temporal form as Lessing would have understood it; the "clock time" of these works is remarkably short. Nor do they unfold events in a homogeneous, linear temporal sequence. The reader may be asked to pass continually from an imagined present to an imagined past, or to integrate innumerable details and see them, as in *Ulysses,* for example, as the components of a single day. The method has been called that of "reflexive reference," and while literature is inevitably a time art in its representation of reality, it need not be framed in the sort of linear, homogenous temporal continuum of time that Lessing assumed as inevitable.

We have passed from the interpretation of literature to the consideration of literary style and genre as themselves interpretations of reality, to the distinction between linguistic and other means of expression or representation. Of course, within the domain of language itself, languages vary in the way in which particular ones "cut up" the continuum of experience. Everyone who translates a foreign language confronts this phenomenon, and Auerbach's contrast between Homeric and biblical styles may well be viewed as manifestation of a deeper contrast than a stylistic one that we may draw between the Greek and Hebrew languages. Here again, biblical scholars would appear to have preceded other humanistic scholars in applying the kind of linguistic analysis that we may be more familiar with through the work of Benjamin Lee Whorf, or Edward Sapir on the languages of American Indians.[13]

Linguistic universalism and a reductive application of the rules of transformational grammar have so dominated modern linguistics, at least in the United States, that a fruitful assimilation of linguistics to the art of interpretation has not progressed as far as we might have hoped. But the utility of modern linguistics for elucidating the problems of interpretation has been amply demonstrated in Hirsch's *Validity in Interpretation* and we may now expect further progress in this direction.

While discussing some of the material I have covered in this essay with a colleague, he called my attention to a poem of Wordsworth, *Upon the Sight of a Beautiful Picture*. It is a superlative poem, although not as widely known as it deserves to be. Since it captures so many of the themes we have been considering and in such brief compass, I cannot resist closing with it and letting the reader interpret for himself.

Upon the Sight of a Beautiful Picture

Praised be the Art whose subtle power could stay
Yon cloud, and fix it in that glorious shape;
Nor would permit the thin smoke to escape,
Nor those bright sunbeams to forsake the day;
Which stopped that band of travellers on their way,
Ere they were lost within the shady wood;
And showed the Bark upon the glassy flood
For ever anchored in her sheltering bay.
Soul-soothing Art! whom Morning, Noon-tide, Even,
Do serve with all their changeful pageantry;
Thou, with ambition modest yet sublime,
Here, for the sight of mortal man, hast given
To one brief moment caught from fleeting time
The appropriate calm of blest eternity.

New Wine in Old Bottles:
Reflections on Historicity
and the
Problem of Allegory

*All of us live in images, even if we go beyond them in philo-
sophical speculation. We might think of them as constituting an
unavoidable myth. . . .*

Karl Jaspers[1]

STUDIES OF ALLEGORY and allegorical interpretation abound and
are by no means confined to the classical *loci* of biblical or
medieval literature. The term "allegory" has certainly become
one for literary scholars to conjure with and, in an extended
sense, has become part of modern critical vocabulary. With
other important critical terms—"romanticism," "classicism,"
"baroque"—it has come to signify a fairly wide spectrum of
phenomena, which upon close inspection would appear to be
quite different one from the other. One confusion which regu-
larly turns up is between allegory as a "style," as a principle of
construction (the author constructs his work to be read allegorically), and allegory as a principle of interpretation (a work is
read allegorically in order to render it acceptable or intelligible
to a later age or a mind foreign to the cultural context of the
work).

Bunyan's *Pilgrim's Progress* is a serviceable example of a
constructed allegory, while the traditional glosses on the Song

of Solomon offer many examples of interpretative allegories. Bunyan, of course, would never have written an allegory without the conviction that the Sacred Text was in great part a divinely constructed allegory, however simultaneously historical and literal the text could be. Dante's allegorism is certainly of a more complex sort than Bunyan's. Although Dante furnishes examples of simple allegorism, modern scholars find it much more illuminating to think of his literary mode as analogous to the "allegory of theologians," an allegory better understood by analogy with biblical typology or figuralism rather than as a substitutive allegory in which something simply stands for something else in the modality of a cipher.

Despite profound differences between Bunyan and Dante, these two writers would have adhered both to a constructive theory of allegory and an interpretative one, and the source for their views in this matter would lie in the long and complex tradition of biblical allegorism. Since our own "secularized" critical versions of allegorical concepts and practices derive from the same tradition, we might briefly glance at the history of such interpretations of Scripture in order to discern the various meanings of allegory and determine precisely what we have conserved, transformed, or discarded from the theological tradition.[2]

From the time of the first allegorizers of Homer, allegory has been described as the kind of discourse in which one thing is understood by another. St. Augustine, the primary educator of the learned Christian world for more than a millenium, so defines it in *De Trinitate*.[3] This definition is, historically, a rhetorical commonplace, but St. Augustine insists that the allegories which the authors of the New Testament found in the Old are not to be understood simply as rhetorical figures. The Old Testament is essentially a historical book, and God foreordained both the events of sacred history and their prophetic inner significance, the later meaning visible to the beneficiaries of the new dispensation.

The first term of this kind of allegorical analogy is a *res,* a reality, whether thing or event, which is also a meaning or sign (*signum*), not a fiction or a purely semantic entity. The second term has the same ontological status. They differ in the place they occupy in the temporal continuum and in bearing a prophetic relationship one to the other. Although this mode of allegorization has commonly been called typological interpretation, the term allegory was traditionally applied to it. It was, however, distinguished from ordinary allegory in that the historicity of the text was neither ignored nor denied.

It is clear that such an exegesis could only have been applied to a sacred text, which gives us the historical foreordination by God of the events of sacred history. If Dante claims to write this allegory of theologians, it is simply because he claims prophetic insight into the divine ordination of events. No one who truly understood this mode of typological historical interpretation would have applied it to Ovid. Such a secular text would certainly have an allegorical meaning in addition to its literal meaning, but only the Sacred Text could have four meanings, since only here are the events themselves signifiers of further events.

St. Augustine, as well as his predecessors in the exegetical art, clearly had in mind St. Paul, for whom the relation between the Church and Synagogue was prefigured in the historical story of Isaac and Ishmael and who found a prefiguration of Christ in Adam and in the Paschal Lamb. Adam is, strictly speaking, a prefiguration through antitype rather than type, for the effect of the man who brought death into the world is cancelled by the death of the man who brought life. The Paschal Lamb is historical in the sense that the sacrifice was enjoined by God upon Israel at a moment of time and the annual sacrifice repeats the historically generated rite. If typology is a historically rooted way of thinking, it can thus serve through the event of rite to return the worshipper to the moment of a divine theophany, to a divine command, and to a perception of its prophetic significance.[4]

With the precedent of St. Paul and the classical traditions of allegoresis, the apostolic fathers and their patristic successors had a ready recourse in their exegetical problems. Had not St. Paul himself used the term and concept of allegory to interpret in Galatians (4:24)? But two quite different tendencies in exegesis emerged from two great centers of Christian intellectual life, Alexandria and Antioch. The Alexandrian fathers,

with the precedents of Philo Judaeus and the markedly hellenized synagogue behind them, developed an intensively philosophical kind of exegesis, to the point of sometimes denying
the literal significance of important portions of Scripture in the
interest of allegorical meaning. None of the Alexandrians, as
Christians, could escape from historicity any more than Philo,
however philosophical, could deny the historical reality of Israel. But some of the exegesis of Origen or Clement, like that
of Philo, is clearly concerned with bringing the Sacred Text
into close harmony with Greek philosophical conceptions of the
divine nature and morality. The universalism of Origen or Clement, in particular Origen's later condemned doctrine of the
salvation of all beings (*apokatastasis panton*), has little biblical
endorsement and is advanced on moral and philosophical rather
than scriptural grounds.

The exegetes of the Antiochan school, Theodore of Mop-
suestia, for example, were far less philosophically oriented, and
while they did not always entirely abandon allegorical and typological interpretation, they gave central importance to the
historical meaning of Scripture, greatly reducing the allegorical
overlay on the text.

St. Augustine and other Latin fathers responded to both
Alexandrian and Antiochan traditions and sought to find a
mean between them. Cassian (*Collationes,* xiv, 8), reinterpret-
ing a formulation of Clement of Alexandria, defined the classic
theory of fourfold allegory which remained normative for theologians throughout the Middle Ages, and for Catholics well
beyond.

There was first the literal sense: what was signified by the
words of the text as such even if the literal sense was conveyed
through figures of speech. The use of an expression such as the
"hand of God" was not, of itself, an indication of allegory but a
simple figure of speech used to describe a divine attribute. Our
own distinction between "literal" and "figurative" is not applicable to this meaning of literal sense. A figurative expression
was still part of the literal sense.

The allegorical sense, *sensu stricto,* was the meaning of an
Old Testament text applied to Christ or to the Church Militant.
The tropological or moral sense applied the text to the soul and

its virtues. The anagogical sense applied the text to heavenly realities. Thus, the psalm *In exitu Israel de Aegypto,* a favorite example which Dante also uses, might be interpreted as follows: the literal sense is simply a reference to Exodus; the allegorical sense might be to Christ as a true Moses whose death and resurrection have led mankind out of bondage; the moral or tropological sense might be the passage of the soul from sin to virtue; the anagogical sense might be the passage of the soul from this world to the heavenly hereafter. Obviously, there is still a good deal of exegetical latitude possible even with Cassian's formula. Nevertheless, the historicity of the method is clear. A historical event from the history of Israel leads to one from the history of Christianity, next to the "history" of the soul in its moral drama, and last to the eschatological reality which sets a term to history.

It is clear this method could not be applied to a secular text penned by a writer uninspired by God. Such a writer could not write of events which are by themselves charged with prophetic meaning, texts in which the realities (*res*) are also signs (*signa*). At the risk of repetition, I would stress that Dante's claim to write a text which requires this kind of exegetical method is essentially a claim to divine inspiration which discloses to his illuminated intellect the transcendent meanings of the real events and figures which fill the fictional frame of the journey. From a less theological point of view, Dante writes a poem in a style analogous to the style of Scriptures, which are *polysemous,* possess plural significations.

To be sure, allegorical exegesis that abstracts from the historicity of the text or leads directly from a text to an abstract philosophical principle was practiced along with allegorical exegesis of the typological kind described in Cassian's normative formulation. Nevertheless, Christian allegorism remained bound to events in the conviction that sacred history was both a system of events and a system of signs, illuminating analogically both the nature of the human soul and its ultimate destiny in time and beyond.[5]

We can now look farther back beyond the Christian dispensation, consider the history of allegorical interpretation in the classical world, and so discern what was taken from that tradition into Christian exegesis and what was largely discarded. From this vantage point we can pass to modern critical conceptions of allegory and consider the outcome of the idea of allegory.

A work attributed to Heraclitus on Homeric problems, probably written in the first century A.D., has survived as the most comprehensive treatise we possess from antiquity on allegorical interpretation.[6] Heraclitus' work is one late response to a conflict present in Greek thought from the time of Plato certainly, but even before in the thought of Xenophanes. The latter was the first Greek thinker to criticize religious myth for not being "fitting" in terms of the true nature of the divine, for not being *theoprepes*. Although he was not the first to coin this word, the word and concept were thus given a new importance for later theological speculation, whether pagan or Christian. Pagan philosophical polemic against its own religious tradition as well as against the new religion of Christianity was based on certain widely shared philosophical conceptions of what the divine nature had to be like. If the behavior of the gods in pagan mythology was blatantly all too human, the polemic against Christianity raised questions concerning whether the Incarnation, the suffering divinity, the anthropomorphic traits of the biblical God, might also not be *theoprepes*.[7]

Both moral and metaphysical reasons dominated the philosophical critique of religion, whether pagan or Christian. The most important statement of this problem is, of course, in Plato's *Republic*, where the philosopher rejects Homer and Hesiod, not essentially as poetic fictions, but as the basis of *paideia*, as works expressing the truths that sound pedagogy requires. Although Plato did not succeed in reforming the traditional basis of education along the lines advanced in the *Republic*, no comprehensive philosophical defense of Homer and Hesiod emerged until the Stoics undertook to defend the poetic works fundamental to Greek education. Indeed, they were defended as expressive of truth, as fit to be retained in the place they occupied as the basis of *paideia*.

At first, the Stoic defense might seem puzzling, for the sages agreed to the conceptions of the divine that were current among the philosophers, that the divine is rational, good, impassive, orderly, holy, above all, not subject to any of the vices or passions of men. Certainly, all men could see that the poets did not, on the face of it, so portray the divine nature. The way out of this dilemma of conserving what was apparently unworthy of conservation was to subject the mythical stories of the ancient classic poets to allegorical interpretation. Only thus could the most prestigious and ancient literature of the Hellenes be safeguarded from the moral, theological, and philosophical censures of a more enlightened age. The Stoics agreed that the poets were either blasphemous or allegorists and they chose, for reasons we shall soon consider, to regard them as allegorists.

A similar problem arose in the history of Judaism and Christianity when some philosophically trained, hellenized believers, were constrained to allegorize the Old Testament along lines very much like those of the Stoic allegorizers of Homer. Philo Judeaus used allegory to harmonize Scripture with Greek philosophical notions of *theoprepes:* where the text says that God spoke to Moses, the text means to say that God illuminated Moses' mind, a clear shift from the naive anthropomorphism of the text to the philosophically hallowed and respectable Greek notion of the illuminated intellect. For Christians, allegorization of the Old Testament saved the text from the extreme moral censure of the God of the Old Testament advanced by Gnostics such as Marcion, who found the Old Testament so objectionable that he wanted to dispose of it altogether. In the case of this conflict, the assumption of allegorical meanings for objectionable texts could conserve the Sacred Text against charges of immorality and crude anthropomorphism. Allegory, in sum, could show that the Bible was really *theoprepes.*[8]

Stoic allegorists had preceded both the Jews and the Christians in finding historical, physical, and moral meanings in the old stories, while the neoplatonists, hard upon the Stoics, had found symbols or mysteries of the transcendent, ideal world in the same place. All through antiquity the rhetorician and the philosopher had offered rival systems of education, posing a conflict between the ideal of the artist with words and philosophic sage, the orator with all the political and literary values that honored title had for Cicero, and the self-transcending seeker of eternal wisdom. The philosophers and their Christian successors discovered in allegorism a way to harmonize the conflict between the authoritative, ancient poetic books and the claims of philosophical reason or rationalized revelation. The pagan philosophers could thus incorporate essential texts of the literary education of their rhetorical rivals without compromising their principles, while the Christians were able to preserve the Old Testament, whether through an extreme form of allegorization prescinding in part from the historicity of the text, or as a typological prophecy.

Heraclitus acknowledges the prima facie validity of the Platonic attack on Homer when he tells us that Homer was apparently the most impious of all men. The stories he tells of the gods and the characters he attributes to them are certainly immoral. Nevertheless, Plato erred in concluding that Homer was to be rejected, for the poet wrote allegorically, which is to speak one thing when one wants to designate another altogether different thing.[9]

Homer wrote this way deliberately, Heraclitus tells us, hiding the noblest truths and his wisdom in the cloak of myths in order to protect the truth from the misunderstandings of the ignorant and thereby render it more beautiful and desirable.[10] We all recognize the merit of these poems, the author implies, for we educate our children with them from childhood. Plato's objections thus cannot stand. He simply did not know how to read Homer. With the allegorical method we can read Homer correctly and learn that there is nothing in his works which could possibly offend the most refined piety and the most delicate moral feelings.

While Plato had acknowledged, at least implicitly, the beauty and power of the Homeric poems while calling into question their suitability for educating the young, Heraclitus takes a totally different tack: the Greeks have in fact been educating their children successfully with these poems for centuries, so Plato is quite simply wrong. Homer merely needs to be read in the right way! Of course, this analysis of the way to read Homeric poems implies a radical distinction between an exoteric, vulgar meaning and a hidden, esoteric one.[11] With this mode of allegorical interpretation the idea of esoteric meaning firmly entered the tradition of exegesis, both secular and sacred. Neoplatonists, pagan and Christian, intent on discovering philosophic meanings in myths and legends, were especially fond of looking down from the heights of their initiation into exegetical techniques upon the vulgar uninitiated, the latter naive enough to think that the texts of Homer or Hesiod were really about what they seemed to be about. The distinction between exoteric and esoteric meanings came to play a remarkable role in the "poetic theology" of the Renaissance neoplatonists who sought a single esoteric system of meaning in the mass of seemingly disparate myths and legends bequeathed to them from antiquity. Such a reading enabled them, too, to attempt a harmonization of pagan and Christian theology in ways the ancient allegorizers of Homer would not have found too surprising.

The problem faced by Heraclitus and his solution are paradigmatic of a recurrent problem in the history of theology and of literary criticism. It is a paradigm of the situation which arose with Jewish Scriptures, the Old Testament in relation to the New, with Virgil in the Middle Ages, and with the Koran after the Arabs absorbed Greek culture. Every one of these texts has been interpreted, in whole or in part, in ways which modern historical consciousness, trained to place beliefs and their expression in a well-defined historical space, can only find absurd or totally irrelevant. Confronted with an exegetical puzzle, we call upon the historian, the anthropologist, the psychologist, the philologist or some other specialist to come to our aid. We ask: what primitive mode of thought might explain the problem? What social practices peculiar to an alien time might explain the strange beliefs enshrined in a text? Our sense of historicity implies a kind of archeology of the mind. Dream processes, neurotic processes, unconscious motives, and symbolizations, the "fossil record" we bear in our psyches, come to play a role in our acts of interpretation along with historical erudition. Allegorization, from one point of view, is the very antithesis of historical interpretation as we understand it now. It is the interpretive device of those with little or no sense that the passage of time truly affects understanding.

Thus, allegorical interpretation becomes a dominant mode of understanding

> when the literal meaning of the sacred books has become questionable but when the giving up of those forms was out of the question, because that would have been a kind of suicide. . . . The reason for their continuation, but with a different meaning attached to them, was not an intellectual but a sociological necessity, having something to do with the fact that continuity of life depends on form— something very hard for the pure intellect, with its historical blind-spot, to grasp.[12]

The essential tradition of the allegorical interpretation of texts not in themselves allegorically constructed is thus normative. Such exegesis is not only in the service of interpreting a text, but is in the service of an institution, a church, or educational system, for which the text is an indispensable *donnée*. Theology cannot call its revelational "given" radically into question without ceasing to exist, any more than the government of the United States can jettison the Constitution, no matter how remote some of its statements be from immediate application now. In certain social and historical contexts, those that Jaeger indicates in his observations, Homer, Virgil, the Bible, a Constitution, all demand interpretation, and even where that interpretation may strike us as remote and forced, we may find the exegetical virtuosity more palatable when we recall that such interpreters were not performing solitary acts of literary criticism, but were dealing with the life-giving forms and traditions of a civilization in a crisis of meaning precipitated by historicity.

Since the Romantic period, we have been assimilating under the rubric of "the intelligible," much that had long remained relegated to the incomprehensible and contingent. The thought forms of children, of the insane, of dreams and fantasy, of hitherto remote and alien cultures, of primitive peoples, all have been studied, and we have satisfied ourselves that we possess some intelligible account of these phenomena. With this armamentarium of modern scholarship, allegorical interpretation is not even remotely necessary, even if we were all committed to some crucial text of a sacred character. But modern interpretation, although it may render the text intelligible, just as surely desacralizes it. The archaic is seen for what it is and not as the cipher of a saving truth. When we hear of psychoanalytic interpretation referred to as a kind of allegorical hermeneutic, we should pause to reflect that the act of interpretation is there not only profoundly individual, but that it reverses the relation between hidden and overt meanings which obtained in the allegorization of the sacred. Where Heraclitus found the most sublime truths and wisdom underneath the crudities of the mythical veil, the psychoanalyst finds the crudities we dare not acknowledge under the generally innocuous, overt hallowed meaning.

Moreover, psychoanalytic interpretation aims at elimination of the archaic, not its conservation. The neurotic, distorted, private text of the individual must yield to a new text which is rational and public. The esoteric meaning is infantile, unclear because it is charged with anxiety, distorted through the psychic agencies of repression. Analysis, in bringing into rational apprehension the archaisms of the psyche, makes the esoteric, hidden meaning exoteric and frees the sufferer from illusion. But illusion, for Freud, is not solely the affliction of the clinically certifiable sufferer from a neurosis or psychosis. Much of the world of culture, religion, and the national state is saturated with illusory beliefs and aspirations. Insofar as psychoanalysis is an unmasking of the absolute claims of culture, the Freudians resemble the Gnostic allegorizers in "blatantly subverting the meaning of the most firmly established, and preferably the most revered, elements of tradition."[13]

The example from psychoanalytic theory is but one modern adaptation of the concept of allegory to uses quite foreign to its origins. Indeed, the term might be applied to mean any interpretation at all: Northrop Frye, for example, says:

> It is not often realized that all commentary is allegorical interpretation, an attaching of ideas to the structure of poetic imagery. The instant that any critic permits himself to make a genuine comment about a poem (e.g., "In *Hamlet,* Shakespeare appears to be portraying the tragedy of irresolution") he has begun to allegorize. Commentary thus looks at literature as, in its formal phase, a potential

allegory of events and ideas. The relation of such commentary to poetry itself is the source of the contrast which was developed by several critics of the Romantic period between "symbolism" and "allegory," symbolism here being used in the sense of thematically significant imagery. The contrast is between a "concrete" approach to symbols which begins with images of actual things and works outward to ideas and propositions, and an "abstract" approach which begins with the idea and then tries to find a concrete image to represent it. This distinction is valid enough in itself, but it has deposited a large terminal moraine of confusion in modern criticism, largely because the term allegory is very loosely employed for a great variety of literary phenomena.[14]

To insist that all commentary is allegory is surely to evacuate the term of all possible precision of reference. More important, it is to confuse reading into a text meanings which often cannot be linked at all to the apparent meaning of the text with the quite different process of extending the significance of the text. In the latter, the literal sense is expanded via precise similitudes, parallelisms, and analogies so as to enlarge what we might call the semantic field of the given text. This enlargement, by establishing relations between the text and similar, more transparent, meanings is what we mean when we speak of clarifying a text. Interpretive commentary in this sense is a special case of the metaphorical process whereby we illuminate X by bringing it into relation with Y, which is similar but somehow better known.

The ancient allegorist who interpreted the figure of Proteus as a mythical expression of the transmutation of elements gave us an arbitrary interpretation. The transmutation of elements is certainly "clearer" and "better known" than the amorphous symbol, but we have no way of deciding which of an unbounded number of transformational processes Proteus could not just as easily signify. The similitude drawn is, in principle, unrestricted, and we are involved in empty analogizing of the kind that follows upon simple binary divisions of the totality of things. If all the world is divisible into active and passive, masculine and feminine principles, then half of all the realities of

the world mean the same thing.[15] It would not do justice to
Angus Fletcher's study of allegory to equate his view with
Frye's, but he, too, seems to confound allegory as a principle
of interpretation with allegory as a principle of construction:

> An objection needs to be met here, namely that all
> romances are not necessarily allegorical. A good adven-
> ture story, the reader will say, needs no interpolated sec-
> ondary meaning in order to be significant and entertaining.
> But that objection does not concern the true criterion for
> allegory. The whole point of allegory is that it does not
> *need* to be read exegetically; it often has a literal level that
> makes good enough sense all by itself. But somehow this
> literal surface suggests a peculiar doubleness of intention,
> and while it can, as it were, get along without interpreta-
> tion, it becomes richer and more interesting if given inter-
> pretation. Even the most deliberate fables, if read naively
> or carelessly, may seem mere stories, but what counts in
> our discussion is a structure that lends itself to secondary
> meaning as well as primary meaning. (*Allegory,* p. 7)

It is difficult to see what could be excluded from allegorical interpretation in this view, since interpretation seems virtually to be conflated with the possibility of a secondary meaning.
The vast bulk of allegorical interpretation that has come down
to us is so "secondary" that no modern interpreter of the
Bible, Virgil, or Homer would dream of using it.

Interpretation, the "meaning of meaning," is surely an act
of great complexity, and it seems especially so in our own time,
for we lack a universally shared, preferred, metaphorical system to which other meanings may be referred. Even theologians, once the possessors of the controlling monomyth, are
constrained to "demythologize" in order to render it intelligible
to an assumed secular intelligence shaped by scientific explanation and a naturalistic view of history. Since Schleiermacher,
some of the finest minds of European culture have dealt with
the problem of general hermeneutics and if ours is a great age
of literary criticism, we surely owe much to him and his successors. One fundamental distinction in this tradition which has
been abandoned only in recent times is the distinction between

the apprehension of meaning and the realization of significance, two associated but distinguishable acts of the mind.[16]

Meaning is associated with the recovery of authorial intention and is not, in principle, an endless task. It is something which we do in every intelligible encounter with the spoken or written word. The apprehension of significance is, on the other hand, unbounded. To say this is simply to point out what we all know. For example, the plays of Shakespeare will remain in some important sense recognizably the same even though the significance of the plays will change. If this were not so we would not have anything like a history of taste in regard to Shakespeare, or, more concretely, the history of Shakespeare criticism. The essential point to grasp is that changing interpretations of Shakespeare, the discovery of new significances in the texts, is not a process of arbitrary change. Each change in significance begins with the apprehension of the meaning of the text and presupposes a nonarbitrary, constant, matrix of meanings which issued out of cognitive, intentional acts of the poet's mind.

If we would understand the difference between meaning and significance, it is important, moreover, to distinguish the different kinds of interpretive acts that different texts constrain us to perform. Emilio Betti distinguishes between a recognitive kind of interpretation which we use for historical and literary texts, presentational interpretation employed for the performance of dramatic and musical texts, and a normative kind of applied interpretation for legal and sacred texts. For Hans-Georg Gadamer, on the other hand, there would seem to be fundamentally only one kind of interpretation, one concerned with finding some kind of application of the text's meaning. His scepticism concerning the possibility of distinguishing between recognitive understanding, interpretation for presentation, and the application of a text's meaning leads him, it would seem, to settle on the last as the essential character of all interpretation. Historicity so affects understanding that anything like Dilthey's act of *Verstehen*—the possibility, resting on the fundamental identity of human nature over all known space and time, of truly bridging the gulf between us and the text—is impossible. We do not, cannot recover authorial intention in our acts of understanding. What we have is some sense of application of the text to our concerns, some contemporary meaning, past which we cannot go. It seems to me, if I understand Gadamer, that his acts of exegesis occur as if we were all jurists or churchmen, interpreting the text for application, but in the absence of the boundaries set by institutions, their traditions of discipline and practice, and their function of regulating human lives. To the interpreter of history or art, the door seems wide open to the proliferation of meanings with no bound.[17]

An example here might be helpful. What, the biblical scholar might ask, did St. Paul mean by the term *pneuma*? If we cannot annihilate the distance which history interposes between us and the Apostle, we can still give a reasonably satisfactory answer to that question with reference to metaphors drawn from the notion of breath to signify a presence of the divine spirit, and so forth. To seek the significance of the concept is to engage in a far more extensive task. What view of human existence does the term imply? What does Paul say with this term concerning God's relation to man? What is the relation of this view to other similar views, past and present. What is man's condition in the world and how does *pneuma* mean to change it? These are, of course, the questions that a biblical theologian might ask, one whose act of interpretation must go beyond meaning to significance.

Interpretation is obviously a permanent necessity of thought whose task is to overcome the remoteness introduced into every human utterance by cultural difference, whether the result of time or geographical difference. But not only are the texts different on which interpretation must bear, the urgency of interpretative acts is also different, and if ancient arbitrariness in interpretation arose from the imperative of conserving the sacred, modern arbitrariness arises from a radical antihistoricism sceptical of the possibility of determining authorial intention and appealing to "existential" truths beyond the occasion of understanding.

To sum up, allegorical interpretation characteristically arises out of the most acute possible crisis in interpretation, when the alternative to making sense of a text—any sense at all—is cultural loss or even cultural suicide. It is not, in the

first instance, a method of construction but a method of conserving supremely authoritative, normative texts when the moral and philosophical changes brought about by historical change
have rendered the apparent meanings of a text either intellectually or morally objectionable.[18]

In such a cultural situation, allegorical exegesis becomes
essentially an act of decoding, however far from authorial intent. It is precisely for this reason that so few of the classic
allegorical readings of Homer, Virgil, or the Bible can even
begin to sound persuasive to modern ears, however attuned we
think we are to what Dante would have called "polysemous"
texts. For Philo Judaeus, the real meaning of various biblical
descriptions of the divine nature is often an utterly different
meaning from the apparent one, a meaning consonant with
Greek philosophical ideals of what the divine nature is like, and
to have excogitated this is to know what the text really means,
something quite different from what it says. The modern
reader, on the other hand, pauses over what the text says and
hypothesizes a cultural era different from our own, thought
processes different from our own, a way of seeing the world
different from our own, and expression valid in its own terms
once we know what those terms are. For the classic allegorist,
the text deliberately hides what it means. The authors presum-
ably wrote in a kind of code, whether to hide the supreme
truths from the gaze of the vulgar or, more generally, to accommodate to the vulgar something of the divine nature in a mode
they might grasp.[19]

Closely bound to a presumed historical meaning of the Old
Testament text, Christian typological exegesis is nevertheless
also a mode of deciphering, although it possesses a kind of
analogical coherence absent from much philosophical and moral allegorizing. The figures and events of the Old Testament
foreshadow those of the New. The events of the New are not in
question, however miraculous and mythical in texture. The
events of the Old transpired as they are described, but a link is
drawn between the Old and New. It may seem remote to us to
draw a typological correspondence between the Flood and
Baptism, but it is a defined relation between the divine way of
using water both to punish and to save. The Christian typolo-

gists are saved from entering the analogical wilderness by the assumption of a preferred referential system, the New Testament, to which a prior referential system is to be referred. Where Philo's referential preference is a system of concepts, Christian typologists possess historical events of a definitive and ultimate character.

From this point of view, to assume that allegorical interpretation is coterminus with interpretation in general is to assume that all texts are codes or like codes in significant ways. Obviously, interpretation is not confined to such procedures as we have been describing or anything very much like them. To interpret Keats' *Ode to a Nightingale* as a complex meditation on art, life, and death is more like an act of translation than an act of decipherment. Nevertheless, all modalities of interpretation are affected by historicity. We have our difficulties in interpreting Homer, but they are of an entirely different order than those which confronted Heraclitus. We can make acts of the informed historical imagination in reading the *Illiad* or the *Odyssey* and seek to overcome what is alien in the work by calling up another time and place as the imaginative matrix of our acts of interpretation. So, too, we need not allegorize the Deuteronomic law for we are quite content to let the pastness of the Bible be pastness. Contrast with an alien past and identification with it so as to overcome its pastness may thus serve understanding.

For the literary scholar, the frequent absurdities and excesses of allegorical exegesis cannot be entirely ignored. The allegorical method of reading Scripture often determined the way in which biblical allusions and citations entered literature. Literary metaphorics and artistic iconography are shaped, often enough, not by what the text said but what the allegorist said it really meant by what it said. Milton, Vaughn, Herbert, not to mention Dante, read their Bible or their classics through an exegetical framework which sometimes makes their manner of allusion seem historically or philologically remote, however successful in its own context.

One profoundly interesting result of the history of Christian exegesis was that, although there grew up a complex system of interpretation of Scripture intelligible in its fullness only

to an intellectual elite, the message of salvation was understood
to be clear, simply accessible to the unlettered and to children.
More than once, St. Augustine tells his reader that although the
Bible is difficult to interpret, what each man needs to know for
his salvation is abundantly clear. For this reason, even for the
sophisticated interpreter, the ultimate exegetical rule is the law
of love.

John Donne in his *Devotions upon Emergent Occasions*
gives magnificent expression to this twofold aspect of Christian
exegesis.

> My *God*, my *God*, Thou art a *direct God*, may I not
> say a *literall God*, a *God*, that wouldest bee understood
> *literally*, and according to the *plaine sense* of all that thou
> saiest? But thou art also (*Lord* I intend it to thy *glory*, and
> let no *prophane misinterpreter* abuse it to thy diminution)
> thou art a *figurative*, a *metaphoricall God too*: A *God* in
> whose words there is such a height of *figures*, such *voy-*
> *ages*, such *peregrinations* to fetch remote and precious
> *metaphors*, such *extensions*, such *spreadings*, such *Cur-*
> *taines* of *Allegories*, such third Heavens of *Hyperboles*, so
> *harmonious eloquutions*, so *retired* and so *reserved ex-*
> *pressions*, so *commanding perswasions*, so *persuading*
> *commandments*, such *sinews* even in thy *milke*, and such
> *things* in thy *words*, as all *prophane Authors*, seeme of the
> seed of the *Serpent*, that *creeps*, thou art the Dove, that
> flies.

Once allegorical interpretation comes into being, the possibility is open for allegory as a principle of construction. Tentatively, I would like to suggest that constructed allegories should
generally be understood as following the typological pattern
rather than the more abstract and unhistorical forms of allegorical exegesis. The works of our literary tradition which demand
to be understood as allegory rather than simply allow allegorical interpretation assume the existence of a central paradigmatic story, of a sacred or near-sacred character, set in the past
and assumed to be historical, or which we are asked to believe
as historical fiction. This story appears as an archetypal pattern
of the story told in the literal sense of the text, and the author,
through metaphor and allusion and, above all, personification,

reminds us of the correspondence between "then" and "now." The archetypal story is the pattern for events of permanent significance repeated now in the life of everyman in an individual mode. What was once "history," whether the Bible, Homer, or Virgil, has now entered memory, been detemporalized and is relived as fictional event in the actions of the protagonist and as spiritual event in the consciousness of the reader. Allegory thus takes account of the historicity of a paradigmatic story, its repeatability as a fiction set in new time and place, and the significance of the history and its corresponding fiction for an analogous spiritual or psychological event taking place in the consciousness of the reader.

The account I have just given is simply a secularized version of how a Christian allegorist working with Christian materials might have proceeded. He might view the Old Testament as *praefiguratio Christi,* the New Testament as *vita Christi,* and the paradigm of the progress of the soul as *imitatio Christi.* His story would be so told as to imply the first two patterns in his account, his "fiction," of the last. Whether in sacred or secularized versions, the works which demand allegorical interpretation seem to be constructed in some such manner. It is no accident that these works are usually cast in the form of a journey, the spatial delineation of nonspatial events, and of a *psychomachia,* the portrayal of critical events and conflicts of the soul as external occurrences.

Even where we seem to be far removed from the sphere of typological thinking, as in the *Roman de la Rose,* we nevertheless find a dominating quasi-mythic pattern, a codified, ritualized pattern of courtship, the archetypal patterns of "proper" lovers. The story which here unfolds as concrete event describes the inner events of a *psychomachia* and it is hard to think of a constructed allegory, Dante's *Divine Comedy* or Spenser's *Faerie Queene,* which does not possess as one tier of its layers of constructed meanings the inner progress and conflicts of the soul. Personification is, after all, the allegorical device par excellence, and when allegory passes from historical, spatially rendered events to signifying the events of consciousness, personification will necessarily be the rhetorical device for relating the two patterns of meaning. Indeed, typological interpretation can often be understood as the taking of "ready-made" persons, as it were, and treating them as both what they were and as personifications of the events of consciousness. The lovers of medieval allegorical romance rarely emerge as individuals but as the bearers of meanings, and where in the Arthurian material, or in the *matière de France,* the text takes on allegorical qualities, some paradigmatic story, often the Christian one, is not far from the author's mind.

Of course, metaphysical doctrines of exemplarism, the doctrine of the signatures of all things, the belief in universal analogies and correspondences, encourage the allegorical or symbolic habit of mind, but true constructed allegory seems to exhibit the typological pattern. In this sense, there is no classical, pagan work of constructed allegory. Parabolic tales, moral fables, exemplary stories abound, but there is nothing demanding the kind of reading we must bring to the *Divine Comedy, The Faerie Queene,* or *Pilgrim's Progress.* Honig's study, *Dark Conceit: The Making of Allegory* (1959), is the most penetrating study of allegory I know and offers a definition of the genre which takes account implicitly of what I have called the typological pattern. He appears to relate allegory to myth in some sense of the term, clearly recognizes the distinction between allegorical and nonallegorical literature, and by defining an "allegorical quality" extends the concept to make it a genre which includes works as disparate as the *Roman de la Rose* and *Rappacini's Daughter, Pilgrim's Progress* and *The Castle, Gulliver's Travers* and *Moby Dick.* The idea of myth appears in his formulation of the "twice-told tale."

> We find the allegorical quality in a twice-told tale written in rhetorical, or figurative, language and expressing a vital belief. In recognizing that when these components come together, they form the allegorical quality, we are on our way to understanding allegory as literature. The twice-told aspect of the tale indicates that some venerated or proverbial antecedent (old) story has become a pattern for another (the new) story. Rhetorical language . . . makes possible the retelling of the old story simultaneously with the telling of the new one. The belief expressed in the tale is the whole idea supporting the parabolic way

of telling and the reason for the retelling. The relating of the new and the old in the reflective nature of both language and theme typifies allegorical narration. The tale, the rhetoric, and the belief work together in what might be called a metaphor of purpose. (p. 12)

Whether the works that Honig brings together as "retellings" should be juxtaposed may sometimes be doubtful, but he does take on the task of what allegory as a principle of construction might specifically imply, and correctly grasps that allegorical construction implies a central, paradigmatic story as reference system, a story taken to be of permanent significance and archetypal in that it must be retold as reapplicable to the present.

The history of allegorism as a principle of interpretation or a principle of construction is intimately bound to the history of myth, whether it has a canonical status or an apocryphal one. The classical myths became our apocryphal important stories when Christianity became the canonical one, and our cultural tradition, richly endowed with two great bodies of myth long considered as antithetic to one another, has afforded interesting examples of allegorical interpretation as a way of reconciling canonical and apocryphal myth. The Platonic theology of Ficino was such an important attempt, with enormous consequences for the use of pagan myth in Christian literature.

Of course, the hypothetical generation of myth creators and myth bearers had no need for exegesis and would not have dreamt of using the myths they bear for "literary" purposes. This myth is fully grasped, entirely lived, and manifested in ritual and in social practice. Allegorical interpretation seeks to preserve the sacral character of myth in the face of a historical progress which makes myth morally and intellectually problematic. Allegorical construction has other characteristics. It implies, to be sure, a certain degree of psychic distance from the naive bearing of myth—the myth becomes usable in fresh contexts and new applications—but the sacral character of the dominent typological pattern is not in question. For the true allegorist, the myth is still in a very important sense history and not pure psychology or simply literature. Whether the modern literary use of myth as we find it in Melville, Mann, Joyce, or

Camus can be said to confer the allegorical quality on their works is problematic. I think not. The mythic background serves to organize and illumine the present material, impose the discipline of form upon it, but it does not, I think, impose on that material a large share of its significance.

Historical scholarship and the growth of historical consciousness have had, after all, the effect of rendering every myth or symbol system unique and somehow valid in its own terms. We assume it is our duty to understand even the most primitive of such constructions from within, to make it usable in itself, however momentarily, as a master image for our own experience. We do not seek simple understanding but sympathetic understanding, to live for a while in someone else's universe. Even classical civilization, the touchstone for centuries of what is "civilized" and what is "barbarous" has become one among many such imaginary cultural universes.

If all myths "work" the result is, of course, that no myth "works." Today the ancient storehouse of myth works essentially by contrast. It is no accident that the mythological allusions in Eliot's *Wasteland* or Joyce's *Ulysses* usually engender ironic or parodistic contrasts between past and present. Not only have great historians and philosophers contributed to this result, but the reinterpretation of the Kantian a priori by modern neo-Kantians has encouraged us to view all mythological, religious, and philosophical systems as models, paradigms, or speculative cosmologies through which we can imaginatively participate, looking at the whole through a perspective provided, so to speak, by someone else's spectacles. The universal a priori which Kant constructed to answer the question of how scientific knowledge is possible has thus been broken up into any number of symbol systems or conceptual structures—the products of history and culture—through which mankind, at a given time or place, organizes the totality of its experience.

If the symbols and frameworks are the filters through which experience must pass, then nothing disconfirming of the framework will ever be recognized. This was an extraordinarily liberating idea. It allowed for the development of anthropology and class oriented social science. Whereas David Hume, a pre-Kantian, could note the reported ideas of American Indians and Africans, he could register them only as strange views of the world; he could not deal with them scientifically. Marx, de Toqueville, Weber, and Durkheim could say the world of the strange people is strange to us, but familiar, comprehensive, and serviceable to them. The very possibility of identifying the study of a culture's *ideas* with the study of *its world* eliminated, in principle if not practice, the otherwise inevitable bias of a person who "really knows" what the objective world is, in contrast to the prescientific savages.[20]

If the growth of historical scholarship and the historical imagination opened the way for us to place the cultures of the past in a well-defined perspective of historical space, the neo-Kantians, generalizing from the master's theory of categories, opened the way for us to view primitive or "exotic" cultures as coherent, effectively complete modes of understanding the world in order to live in it. Since a work conditioned by time, or from a foreign remote culture, implies a coherent whole, a symbolic cosmos, we are never driven to make acts of allegorical interpretation.[21] We are no longer required to translate everything that time or distance has rendered strange to us into our own preferred mythology or into the presumed objectivities of a system of philosophy or natural science. With such a perspective at our disposal, allegorical exegesis had to die. Perhaps we now wait for a Hegel who will attempt to tell us what the whole is which we glimpse in all those parts we are asked to experience as wholes. Such a person would write for us a new and more encompassing phenomenology of the spirit.

The Platonic Debate over
Myth, Truth, and Virtue

*In a sense the history of Greek culture is the history of its
attitudes to myth; no other important western civilization has
been so controlled by a developed mythical tradition.*

G. S. Kirk[1]

IN SOME ENORMOUSLY INFLUENTIAL passages of the *Republic,*
Plato attacks poetry on two grounds, one moral and the other
metaphysical. The poets, he said, Homer and Hesiod in particular, tell immoral and unworthy stories of the gods. They do
not give a true picture of the divine nature and appeal to our
base passions rather than to that which is highest in us. Moreover, poetry imitates or represents a reality—that reality available to the senses—which is but a copy of true reality, the ideal
world of forms lying beyond space and time and available only
to reason.

With surprisingly little change, Plato's critique has re-
curred in substance or been revived *eo nomine* in Western
thought. In the Middle Ages, the poet's antagonist was the
philosophical theologian rather than the philosopher. St. Thomas, for example, recognizing that both poetry and theology use
figurative language, defines poetry as that branch of knowledge
with the minimum of truth, where the figures are but pleasur-
able adornments, while the metaphors of the Sacred Text are
the result of a divine accommodation to the limitations of the
human intellect. If poetry and theology seem to be formally

similar, they are nevertheless at the opposite ends of the spectrum of the knowable.[2]

St. Thomas' views on this matter are of great importance in the long history of the "wars of truth," for he adapts the Platonic argument to the needs of Christian theology. Revelation is, in great part, given to us in figurative terms. The sceptic might simply conclude that revelation is simply poetry and myth. After all, pagan philosophical polemic against both Christianity and its own mythological tradition had been at pains to point out that many of the beliefs and expressions enshrined in Scripture were identical in form and content to beliefs held by pagans and that the philosophical critique of religious myth applied with equal force to both the pagan and the Christian mythology.[3]

It was thus of the highest importance for the defenders of Christianity to separate what looks like poetry and myth, but isn't, from what actually is poetry and myth. If poetry and theology seem similar in their use of figurative discourse, they are nevertheless totally different in the reference of their language. The figurative language of revelation is thus clearly separated from the figurative language of poetry and from the abstract, rational statements of philosophy. This division is clear, although what for St. Thomas was literal would for us have entered the realm of the poetic or mythological.

Poetry also found its defenders. Not only does Aristotle answer the Platonic strictures on poetry, but the Plato of the *Phaedrus* and the *Symposium* could be turned against the Plato of the *Republic*. Aristotle defends poetry as giving us truth, indeed a higher truth than history for it offers us the universal in the particular while history gives us simply the particular. Whatever Aristotle means precisely by "catharsis," it is clear that this concept of the "purgation" or "purification" of the emotions which tragedy engenders is a defense of the passional aspect of poetry. Whether "catharsis" means getting rid of something unhealthy or the purification of raw emotions by raising them to a more acceptable or intelligible level, Aristotle clearly has Plato in mind, for his teacher had found a danger in the unworthy tales told of the gods, especially in the appeal such stories made to our baser, passionate nature. Aristotle thus defends both the intellectual and the emotional side of poetry against the Platonic attack. Emotions, as we experience them in viewing the great tragedians, are experienced in a valuable way, and we learn something of universal significance as we watch the drama unfold.

The *Phaedrus* doctrine of poetry as the product of a divine madness, a *theia mania,* led to the idea that poetic metaphor and the myths of poets might well refer to transcendental truths, from which realm of being the poet's inspiration derives. Truths expressed in the forms of poetry might not otherwise be available to us. This positive view of poetic discourse found its spokesmen from time to time even in the Middle Ages, notably with Dante, and became a dominant strain of literary theory during the Renaissance with the revival of the study of the *Phaedrus* and *Symposium.* Indeed, the poetic theology of both the ancient and Renaissance neoplatonists is, from one point of view, simply a theory of accommodative metaphor applied to extra-biblical sources. A Christian neoplatonist was likely to give the metaphorical, mythical, and symbolic systems of Christianity a preferred referential status, but ancient myth and poetry also could refer to the transcendent, and contemporary poets might thus advance quite seriously their claims to the possession of "higher" truths.[4]

Indeed, the neoplatonic revival of doctrines of symbolic truth led to some of the most extraordinary as well as influential exegetical principles in the history of interpretation. Edgar Wind's penetrating observations on neoplatonic exegesis emphasizes their peculiarity:

> The belief that because a thing is not stressed it must be important is not entirely without merit but it can lead to exegetic madness. Gibbon ridiculed a faith which taught its adherents that a "contradictory doctrine *must* be divine since no man alive could have thought of inventing it." By the same token it is a prejudice to assume that a thing must be central because it looks marginal. On the other hand, the supposition that some things which look marginal *may* be central is one of those judicious reflections which rarely fail to open up new fields because they introduce a change of focus. Not only is it true that great dis-

coveries have generally "centered" around the "fringes" of knowledge, but the very progress of knowledge may be regarded as a persistent shift of center. In Cusanus and Pico, a sharp instinctive awareness of the rule that any given knowledge may be transcended was condensed into a mystical superstition: a belief that all important truths are cryptic. But from this bleak, retardative axiom of faith, perhaps the most perilous vestige of neoplatonism, they drew a prophetic rule of learning: that it is more profitable to explore the hidden bypaths of knowledge than to tread the common highways. Enlightenment and obscurantism were tightly linked in the method of the *docta ignorantia*.[5]

The obscurantist strain flowed, oddly enough, from that character of Renaissance neoplatonism which made is so appealing to the cultivated minds of the period: it obliterated all of the major distinctions in the morphology of knowledge so carefully established in the scholastic tradition. Pagan and Christian symbolism, humanistic and scientific learning, all could flow together, for all knowledge is ultimately symbolic and revelatory of the transcendent. The "many" is but a tissue of metaphors, symbols, figurations, of the "One." And if all knowledge thus constitutes a revelation, then all revelations may also be one. This last conviction was expressed in the notion that revelation had been given through a succession of sages (some actually historical and others assumed to be historical figures although we now know they were not): Plato, Moses, Orpheus, Hermes, Zoroaster, and Christ.

Examples of neoplatonic exegesis might illustrate Wind's observations. An excellent example is the neoplatonic interpretation of the birth of Venus. Aphrodite arises from the formless matter from which all things arise and which is symbolized by the sea. In Hesiod's account in the *Theogony*, the foam of the sea is equated with the semen of Uranus, released when this sky god was castrated by his son. The semen represents the celestial form giving principle which shapes the formless, earthly, material principle. Clearly, we are meant to discern the metaphysical relation of matter and form behind the story. This interpretation could also have been made consonant with the scientific account of generation offered by Aristotle. The male semen, for Aristotle, was the vehicle of a *pneuma,* akin to the heavenly creative heat of the sun, which shaped the embryo after the semen amalgamated with the passive, female blood. Of course, to a modern psychoanalyst, the crude myth is really interesting for other reasons and scarcely disguises the wish to castrate the father and its conflation with childhood fantasies concerning the sexual relations of parents.

The cruder the myth, it sometimes seems, the more philosophical the interpretation. The dying, dismembered, and reborn gods of late antiquity—Osiris, Attis, Adonis—all were given a common interpretation. The fate of these gods signified the cosmogonic process of emanation from the One, the "dismemberment" of the supreme unity into multiplicity, and the timeless return of that multiplicity to the primordial unity. The bloody stories became symbols of a cosmogonic death and rebirth, and all the analogous myths thus had a common philosophical meaning.

"Platonic theology," "poetic theology"—such phrases describe thought as symbolic and imply the universalism which flows from such a conception of knowledge.[6] In principle, if not always in practice, Christian symbolism had lost its exclusive, preferred status. It had become subject to syncretistic amalgamation with other systems of myth and symbol, all in turn symbolic indices of a reality beyond definitive expression. Such universalism is closer to philosophical perspectivism—each symbol system affording a view or perspective of the whole—than to the reduction of all systems of thought to a single one which contains the truth of the rest and renders them obsolete.

Universalism of the second sort is found in the modern psychoanalytic theory of myth. All myths translate or "reduce" to the one great childhood family story—so the Freudians—or all myths translate into the universal psychic process of individuation and harmonization of the divergent and conflicting aspects of the psyche; the latter view, of course, is Jung's. For Freud, myths reflect the archaic world of childhood wishes and fears, while for Jung they are directly symbolic of the very character and structure of the psychic process. In either case, the view of myth is universalistic but reductive. There is essentially only a "monomyth."

That modern school of biblical exegesis inaugurated by Rudolf Bultmann offers a third possible treatment of myth, which goes by the name of "demythologizing." While theology has long been concerned with rationalizing and interpreting the data of revelation, Bultmann's approach seems distinctive in the manner in which myth is simultaneously almost eliminated and conserved. From Bultmann's point of view, the theologian demythologizes the text in the interest of an existential significance. He cannot, or should not, reduce the myth or totally eliminate it in the interest of a purely naturalistic, secular interpretation. The work of the theologian is not like that of the scientist or the philosopher, although Bultmann acknowledges the claims of science and may use the concepts of the philosopher to elucidate the attitude toward existence behind its mythic expression. Neither can the theologian treat his preferred myth simply as an instance of the universal truth, or a perspective upon the transcendent, capable of amalgamation to other religious myths, without ceasing to be the theologian of any religion in particular. Possessing through faith a preferred myth of universal significance, he must acknowledge the mythical elements in it, demythologize the sacred story but nevertheless conserve it. How is this possible?

Despite all the archaic and primitive features of the Christian story, there is an attitude toward existence enshrined in it. The demythologizer elucidates that view of life and its solution to the problem of existence. This is possible for Bultmann because the mythic is merely an outworn cosmology which modern science and historical scholarship have rendered obsolete. It is the vocabulary of another time applied to talking about the beyond in this-world terms. The three-tiered universe of heaven, earth, hell, the causation of illness through demonic agencies, miraculous interventions in the normal course of events, the dead rising out of the grave, all these are features of an archaic cosmological language through which the men of a certain time and place conveyed their understanding of life, of the problems of existence, and of what man must do to confront them. The myth tells of man's existential situation in the world, of the problematic character of existence, *through* its archaic manner of expression. In one sense, then, the biblical story cannot be used as evidence for "faith" in the sense of providing "objective" evidence for special beliefs. Nevertheless, *through* if not *in* the myth, we may find faith as that particular way of being in the world that the myth conveys. We may, in finding a unique solution to the problem of existence, acquire authentic existence.

On the other hand, demythologizing is only one aspect of the religious life. The concrete life of religion—liturgy, worship, prayer—remain rooted in the particular mythology. Bultmann is far from wanting to demythologize the Lord's Prayer or the Psalms and great hymns of the Lutheran liturgy. His sermons, often very moving in their piety, are written in the traditional language of religion; one who reads them would scarcely suspect how sceptical Bultmann the scholar is about knowledge of the historical Jesus, or miracles and the whole apparatus of traditional supernaturalism. The religious life must remain rooted in its mythical and symbolic traditions, while the reflective believer is also constrained to transcend it by demythologizing revelation. The religious life remains particular and committed to its preferred referential system—its "revelation"—but renders it universal through interpretation.

Bultmann has been attacked both by those more sceptical than he and by those more committed to conventional piety. He has been accused of reducing religion to an instance of Heidegger's philosophy. He has also been accused of inconsistency in wanting to keep the whole symbolic and mythical apparatus of Christianity at the same time as he appears to render it obsolete. Is Bultmann's theology but one more example of myth for the unlettered masses and philosophy for the intellectual believer, of an exoteric Christianity which is mythical and an esoteric Christianity which is conceptual and cast in the terms of existentialism? I think not. In his own terms he has worked out, in the sphere of epistemology, the uttermost consequences of the Lutheran doctrine of justification by faith alone. His philosophical vocabulary no more swallows up the religious element in his thought than did the vocabulary of St. Thomas in his theological work. Bultmann's intellectual task was to remove from religion those peculiar claims of objectivity so vulnerable to the criticisms of historical, philosophical, and scientific thought. Indeed, he stands in some important ways in the Platonic tradition of the critique of religious myth. Such myth is not everywhere intellectually or morally *theoprepes,* "befitting of the divine," and if Bultmann cannot invent his own myth, he can disclose the Christian myth's value for the religious life. Religion is not subsumed into philosophy, for religion cannot achieve expression in that mode of universality available to abstract thought. Through the exegetical method of demythologizing, however, the particular modalities of religious life can be raised to the level of universality.

Religious myth and scientific or philosophical thought are always in contrast if not at war with one another, and Bultmann stresses, perhaps more than necessary, the role of modern science in profoundly altering what we might call the "believability index" of revelation. Karl Jaspers correctly pointed out that many ancient thinkers found Christian myth quite unbelievable well before anything like modern science or modern scientific historical scholarship appeared. Nevertheless, I think that Bultmann is correct in locating the present exegetical crisis in the extraordinary transformation of our lives, intellectually and practically, that the development of modern science has brought about. Belief has always been a problem for some and sometimes for many, but Bultmann's view of a "believing" interpretation relates it to a larger crisis which obtains within humanistic culture in general and its relation (or lack of relation) to the scientific culture. Modern discussions on the relation of the poetic-mythic imagination and its claims to truth are more likely to arise in controversies concerning "two cultures" than in theological debates.[7]

The relation—to borrow W. H. Auden's expression—between the "Grand Dukes of Science" and "the shabby curate of poetry" is not everywhere gracious but not everywhere hostile either. It is marked by some degree of acknowledgment on both sides of the insufficiency of either an exclusively scientific or literary culture. Yet, modern discussion for the most part falls well below the level set by Arnold, Huxley, and Mill in the nineteenth century and scarcely suggests any profound awareness of the crucial cultural and interpretative problems implied in the subject. The question turns on what sort of moral insight and knowledge does the poetic imagination give us and how adequate is this body of knowledge as *paideia*? How does science, the most portentous intellectual movement of modern times, limit or affect our relation to literary and humanistic culture?

This brief account of the persistence and vitality of the problems raised by Plato in the *Republic* may serve to take us back to a more extensive analysis of the Platonic argument itself. In Books two and three (376E–412B) of the *Republic* Plato considers the desirability of censoring literature in the educational curriculum. The system in need of reformation was general in Athens and, insofar as it was humanistic, had as its basis the thorough study of the poems of Homer and Hesiod. Despite the differences between Greek religious attitudes and those of modern times, it would not be entirely inappropriate to see their role as analogous to the role of the Bible in the educational systems of Western civilization until recent times. Arising, like the Bible, from a long past world, the Homeric poems enshrined still current ideals of Athenian culture—the bravery of Achilles, the cleverness and resourcefulness of Odysseus— at the same time preserving a theology which attributed to the gods all manner of evil conduct and immorality. Philosophic criticism of the received religious tradition had begun well before Plato with the pre-Socratics, and Xenophanes, as we have seen, four generations earlier had sharply attacked the revered theological-poetic legacy for the immoral acts attributed to the divine nature.

By the time of Pericles, the educated Hellene no longer believed in the actual, literal existence of the ancient divinities. In itself, disbelief of this sort did not pose any grave political or cultural threat. Religion had a civic and ritual character rather than a doctrinal one. It was supported by the state, and an official priesthood simply carried out the traditional rites and celebrations without demanding explicit belief, much less formulating dogmatic propositions to which one had to assent. The political authorities would have objected, of course, to any vociferous or strident denial of the existence of Zeus or Hera or Athena or Apollo, but the state would not have dreamt of enforcing any kind of intellectual religious conformity. It was

quite possible for a scholar and thinker to observe the rites of
the official religion while giving to the myths and legends interpretations more consonant with a rational and moral outlook or
even quietly dismissing the myths altogether.

It should not surprise us, therefore, that Plato nowhere
proposes any radical reconstruction of traditional religion. He
freely uses the plural "gods" or the singular "god" to suit his
fancy, and even the neuter "the divine" appears interchange-
ably with the personal noun. He does not discuss whether and
to what degree the gods are to be understood literally. They are
assumed to exist in some sense, and critique of the traditional
religion is confined to the immorality of the stories men invent
about the gods and not to the gods as they might be assumed to
be in themselves.

Plato's philosophical theology leads directly to a kind of
monotheism, but surely allows for the existence of a plurality
of divine natures. This, of course, left ample room for his fol-
lowers to give adequate philosophical interpretations of the
gods of mythological tradition: they are metaphysical principles
subordinate to the one, or they are purely spiritual intermediary
beings, "daimons." Plato's first concern, the moral critique of
poetic myth, raises a fundamental theological problem: can we
attribute to the divine nature characteristics which would be
called evil if attributed to men? Mill's powerful critique of such
Christian teachings as the idea of everlasting torment of the
damned is rooted in this ancient perception of the problem.

Before continuing with Plato's critique of myth on moral
grounds we should pause to note that the problem of what is
befitting of the divine nature is in some respects more acutely
posed within Judaism and Christianity than within Greek poly-
theism. To be sure, in Plato the individual gods of the mythic
tradition must be freed of any inputation of evil and immoral
actions. But beyond them lies a wholly transcendent Good, a
supreme divine reality which transcends gods, men, and the
whole of the universe of space and time. It is beyond being and
in some sense the *arche* or ultimate origin of all reality, but it is
not really possible to predicate anything very much of it except
its "goodness." Like the sun of the physical world, it shines in
that other world, illuminating the "distance" between the truth

and the intellect. Although the ultimate of realities, the Good is essentially inactive and we cannot make moralistic judgments about an activity it does not exercise.

In ethical monotheism the question of the moral character of the divine nature is far more complex and relentlessly paradoxical. A foremost modern student of ancient Judaism, writing from within the tradition itself, has aptly described the peculiarity of this problem:

> It is true that historical monotheism aspired to raise morality to the level of supreme law. Abandoning the amoral universe of magical forces it conceived the idea of a moral cosmos, whose highest law is the will of God. But this idea arose out of monotheism, and not the reverse. One can discern, therefore, a primary non-moral or supramoral element in monotheistic faiths: the will and command of God is absolutely good. The doctrine of predestination held by some Christian denominations is the most striking form of this idea. God has foreordained who will be saved and who will be damned. At this point the absolute will of God becomes in essence immoral; monotheism approaches paganism. What is important in the present context, however, is the fact that exaltation of the One made it possible for cruelty to develop on a religious basis. God's glory, name, the sacra become the highest values; an offense against them is the supreme crime which justifies any punishment. Israel devoted the enemies of YHWH to destruction; Christianity destroyed idolators and heretics for the glory of God; Islam fought holy wars. Precisely because of its exclusiveness monotheism can be ruthless. . . .
>
> Some of the legends that lay demonic activity to God (such as the attack upon Moses in Exod. 4:24) are to be viewed as the outcome of the monotheistic tendency to refer every event to YHWH—even such as would formerly have been ascribed to demons. The folk religion evidently took no offense at this notion, and something of this view is retained in biblical literature. . . . While it is axiomatic that sin is man's doing, the religious consciousness of the Bible was unable to reconcile itself entirely with this restriction of God's dominion. There is a tension here between the moral demand that sets limits to the

working of God and the religious demand that subjects all to divine control.[8]

Plato's formulation of the moral problem escapes the extreme dilemma that Kaufmann so lucidly describes. The unitary divine principle in Plato is not a will or a person, and the gods, however good they should be understood to be, are themselves subordinated to a source which transcends all realities, human or divine. Hence, the moral criticism of myth leads directly into the metaphysical implications of myth and poetry later in the *Republic* (X, 595A–608B). Plato's second attack deals with the status of poetry and myth as knowledge and is addressed in the first instance to those contemporary sophists and rhapsodes who claimed that all kinds of useful knowledge of truth, as well as a complete code of moral and religious conduct, could be found in the Homeric poems and even in the tragedians. The second critique, like the first, is directed less to poetry per se than to the use of the traditional texts as the basis of the educational system.

The claims of the proponents of "poetic" education might strike us as extravagant. Not only did Homer suffice for shaping a good ethical agent and citizen, he offered valuable instruction in practical matters like chariot driving or military strategy to boot. Similar claims might be familiar to those who know a little about the so-called Bible colleges scattered here and there in the United States. If they are less practical in their claims on behalf of Holy Writ, they are equally convinced that it offers a complete guide to conduct in this life and to bliss in the hereafter.

Plato's criticism of these claims is well known. True reality is accessible only to reason and only after a severe moral and intellectual discipline. The inferior reality accessible to sense is not the domain of truth but of "opinion." Any artist, in imitating a reality which is itself only an imitation of true reality, takes man even farther away from the essential form of things and the truth than he already finds himself to be. Moreover, the appeal of dramatic poetry is to the emotions and not to reason. Such works encourage us to experience all kinds of unworthy feelings that corrupt character. The only poetry which does no harm is that which confines itself to praising virtue and good men. We may assume, of course, that even poetry with morally sound subject matter does not escape the metaphysical stricture of being twice removed from reality or of appealing to lower emotional faculties even when it praises the right things. Clearly, poetry is scarcely worthy of the highest dedication. With this analysis, Plato drew the sharpest possible division between the work of reason and the work of the poetical and mythical imagination.

Plato's attitudes toward myth were by no means unambiguous, at least in the view of his many interpreters. If, indeed, the Homeric tales of the gods are untrue and immoral, may not myth give us an account of subjects of highest importance that we might not otherwise be able to consider? The doctrine of love attributed to Diotima in the *Symposium,* the creative work of the Demiurge in the *Timaeus,* the pre-existent life of the soul in the *Phaedrus,* all these and more of the great themes of Platonic thought are given to us in mythic discourse. To be sure, myth can give us only a probable account of the realities it deals with, a kind of "as-if" story, but perhaps this is the only account we can have short of the pure intellectual vision available only to the philosopher at the end of his arduous quest. And of that, if Plato's *Seventh Letter* represents him correctly, the philosopher cannot talk at all.

The bringing of cosmos out of chaos, the nature and goal of love, the life and destiny of the soul are complex subjects at the limit of knowledge, subjects not readily cast in the forms of discursive reason. But myth is certainly the language of relations and values, and we might hope that it can delineate structures of reality not otherwise apprehensible. Certainly the ultimate mode of knowledge will transcend all symbolic mediation including language, but myth may be a valuable and even indispensable instrument of the philosophic quest just as discursive reason is at another stage. Plato thus offers us a view of myth as the product and the object of philosophic reflection and insight. The limitations of mythic thinking are, from this point of view, simply the limitations of the mind in dealing with the extreme problems of thought. Myth is thus a matrix of meanings which upon reflection yields insight, understanding, and intuition into the structure of reality.[9]

Such a positive view of myth should not be confused with

the ancient theory of myths as encoding an esoteric wisdom which the initiated exegete makes plain at will to his disciples. In Plato's view, myth is not a code. It may be transcended but only in the sense that man is capable of rising to the level of possessing unmediated knowledge, knowledge that goes beyond the instrumentalities of language. Those admirers of Plato who have found this a view of myth in his work are usually cognizant, like Plato himself, of the inadequacies of language. Whitehead tells us: "One source of vagueness is deficiency of language. We can see the variations of meaning, although we cannot verbalize them in any decisive, handy manner. Thus we cannot weave into a train of thought what we can apprehend in flashes . . . . For this reason, conventional English is the twin sister to barren thought. Plato had recourse to myth."[10]

At times we surely find in Plato the use of myth as "a necessary means of freeing the individual from his own whims and fancies," even though in the individual's knowledge of the Good he is in turn freed from the limitations of myth. The same Plato who found the old traditional myths unsatisfactory and who witnessed decay of the religious traditions of his country, created fresh myths which express the conviction of man's overriding relation to the Good, his relation to a transcendent world which is both his origin and his destiny. Such a commanding sense of the singular goal and origin of life cannot really be satisfactorily or persuasively expressed purely in terms of abstract propositions. The myths therefore tell stories of the pre-existence of the soul, of its nature and origin, of the journey it must take, of its fall from its true state. To adopt the mythic mode is to tell all that one can of a reality which cannot be directly grasped and which is far richer than can be conveyed in the language of abstractions. Myth, on the other hand, is certainly not the last resting place of the mind in its quest for the Good. It is the Good which will in turn free us from the limitations of myth and, indeed, of language and ratiocinative thought itself.[11]

Less philosophical students do not find Platonic myths to be heavily charged with philosophic meanings.

> Myths in which dilemmas are apparently resolved, rather than being sanctified or overlaid, seem more exciting to

modern critics, since they appear to exemplify a possible approach to problems of the kind that even we, with greater resources of knowledge and logic, cannot begin to solve. Yet this is, of course, an illusion. When philosophers like Plato have recourse to myth, at those crucial points at which pure reason seems unable to advance further, the kind of myths they choose are not those that faintly foreshadow, or short-circuit, the methods of philosophy. They are purely evocative and imagistic, asserting the truth of immortality and the like by reference to jewel-studded hills or lands flowing with milk and honey. In a way the Epic of Gilgamesh, and genuine myth in general, does better. It is rarely just wish-fulfillment, and the primary myth maker may be said to stand closer to reality than does the philosopher who uses myth as second best.[12]

The contrast in these views is certainly itself Platonic. As on so many issues, Plato is his own best critic. If myth is not, as Whitehead thought, a necessary philosophical escape from the constrictions of conventional language, some of the myths of Plato are by no means purely evocative. The *Timaeus* myth and the myth of the state in the *Republic* are surely to be understood as models or paradigms. The world is to be understood as something made. Since justice is the political virtue par excellence, we are asked to see what we can learn about it by constructing a fictive state embodying some comprehensive definition of justice. Knowing is something like remembering, and loving is more like the re-finding of a once loved object than of loving something utterly new. Let us then construct a speculative cosmology framing the soul's history and see what such intuitions might imply about its nature. So might an explanation of the recourse to myth in the *Phaedrus* run. If the primary myth maker stands closer to reality than the philosopher who uses myth when ordinary language fails, the reality in question is certainly totally different from the reality Plato had in mind. And our evaluation of the philosophic uses of myth, and of myth in general, will depend on our metaphysics and on our view of symbolic expression.[13]

After all, myth is ineluctably a stimulus to philosophical reflection if only because of the matters with which it deals. What are the gods like? Why do men suffer, age, and die? Can man expect to be immortal? How is the world of man related to the surrounding world of nature? This last problem, a major theme of myth, entered the Greek philosophical tradition in the form of long debates over the physis-nomos antithesis, the conflict between what is true or right by nature and what by convention. In such a manner, mythical and religious conceptions have often served to generate, in "secularized" form, philosophical concepts. Hegel's ultimate passage of thought from art to religion to philosophy, the last of which incorporates and transcends the lower stages, is not without its truth even if we reject his metaphysics.

Perhaps the most interesting question in modern speculation on myth is its autonomy. Is myth an autonomous mode of mental functioning, an indispensable activity of the mind not capable of "reduction" or complete translation into other modes of mental functioning? Does the case for irreducibility obtain even if we agree that myth is somehow archaic or primitive and stands in need of rationalization? Carl Jung, for example, believed that myth making and myth believing performed a psychologically adaptive function, virtually a biological one. Myth is the unique vehicle of experiences not otherwise obtainable which serve to integrate the psyche and bring man into harmony with himself and his environment. In this respect it serves a therapeutic function, and the "truth" of myth is essentially psychological and demonstrated in its healing efficacy. Certainly myth, like all the other phenomena of the mind, is subject to analytical understanding, but we do not ask for its truth as we do in the realm of philosophy. Jung was given, of course, to the mythic personification of psychic processes and functions, and this permitted him to deal with myth as a psychobiological function expressive of the deepest layers of mental life, a life older and, in a sense, "wiser" than that abstract reason which was the last psychic power to emerge in the long course of human evolution.

Certainly, if the interpreter takes the view that myth is an autonomous activity of the mind not capable of complete translation, it will markedly affect the way he interprets myth. A rationalistic, reductionist interpreter of myth, for example, will view the old Mesopotamian myths as "prelogical" ways of viewing natural phenomena and will interpret them as nature allegories. That is, he will substitute abstract and conceptual formulations for the myth's personifications and symbols. On the other hand, the interpreter who views myth making as an autonomous and irreducible function of the mind will be aware that the Mesopotamian poets and storytellers thought of the world in a form which is prior to any distinction between the myth and its abstract interpretation. Rationalizing allegory can only come into being when we are aware that there are two ways of talking about the same thing, the one conceptual and the other symbolic.

A rationalist, even if he believes that men are incurably oriented towards myth, will inevitably interpret myth as an archaic way of looking at things which we can now view in the dry light of scientific reason. The myth maker is a dreamer but one who is wide awake while he dreams. The stuff of myth is interpreted, transcended, but dismissed as a primitive mode of mental functioning. Other interpreters, autonomists of one kind or another, are generally struck by the inexhaustibility of myth, the many meanings and relations which can be read out of it, apparently in an unbounded way. Myth may thus be, even if archaic in some sense, a unique way of expressing aspects of experience *totum simul,* aspects which would not hang together in conceptual form. Myth thus gives faithful expression to the paradoxical, contradictory, valuational aspect of human experience.

Indeed, for Cassirer, myth is the primary way in which man renders his experience intelligible. It is the symbolic expression of significance as initially grasped and thus constitutes a matrix of meanings. Rational process then may work on mythic material and derive conceptual structures. But the myth is in essence inexhaustible and the making of myth necessary and unavoidable. For both Jung and Cassirer myth always remains at least partly inviolable, always somewhat mysterious and somewhat inapproachable.[14]

One often misses from discussions of Platonic myth, and even from discussions of the literary use of myth, any consideration of style. The primary myth maker may not be interested in it, but surely the philosophic or literary user of myth must be concerned with it. A myth we recognize as beautiful and rich in meanings must certainly have economy, lucidity of adaptation of means to ends, in relation to style. I use style in the larger sense that Whitehead gave to the term in a remarkable passage in his *The Aims of Education:*

> The sense for style . . . is an aesthetic sense, based on admiration for the direct attainment of a foreseen end, simply and without waste. Style in art, style in literature, style in science, style in logic, style in practical execution have fundamentally the same aesthetic qualities, namely, attainment and restraint. The love of a subject in itself and for itself, where it is not the sleepy pleasure of pacing a mental quarter-deck, is the love of style as manifested in that study. Here we are brought back to the position from which we started, the utility of education. Style, in its finest sense, is the last acquirement of the educated mind; it is also the most useful. It pervades the whole being. The administrator with a sense of style hates waste; the engineer with a sense for style economizes his material; the artisan with a sense of style prefers good work. Style is the ultimate morality of the mind.[15]

If I may adapt the title of one of Lévi-Strauss' books, the anthropologist may well prefer his myths raw, but artists and philosophers like them cooked. It is the reshaping of myth to actualize its latent intellectual and aesthetic content which makes the myths of a Plato memorable. His reconstruction of Orphic and cosmogonic stories saturates the raw material of myth with intelligible content. Hence we discern in his mythical imagination evidence of the same creative power with which Aeschylus and Sophocles raised the old, crude stories of tradition to the heights of eloquence, aesthetic power, and intelligibility. If style is the ultimate morality of the mind, eloquence is the ultimate mannerliness of the mind, the rendering of the detailed fine structure of significance.

Classic expression was given to the superiority of mythic expression over abstract expression by "Romantic" scholars such as Bachofen. For him the mythic is really the symbolic in that exalted sense that Schelling or Coleridge gave to the term. In Bachofen, "the symbol" means the "mythological symbol."

The symbol [i.e., mythological symbolism] awakens intuition where the language of abstraction can only offer rational explanation. The symbol addresses every side of the
human spirit, whereas the language of abstraction is bound
to confine itself to a single thought. The symbol strikes a
chord in the very depths of the soul, whereas the language
of abstraction touches only the surface of the mind like a
passing breeze. The one is directed inwards, the other
outwards. Only the symbol can combine a wide variety of
notions into a single total impression; the language of abstraction, on the other hand, arranges them in succession
and presents them to the mind piecemeal, whereas they
ought to be presented to the soul at a single glance. Words
reduce the infinite to finitude, symbols lead the spirit beyond the bounds of the finite into the infinite world of
abiding truth.[16]

In the last analysis, myth is subject to a twofold exegesis
within the Platonic tradition. One eliminates the myth and the
other conserves it, either by decoding it into something acceptable or conserving it as a form of knowledge. These two tendencies find their parallels in our own time. Freud, Marx, and
Nietzsche, the great unmaskers of myth, see the interpretation
of myth as diminishing illusions, for myth is the mask that man
places on his wishes, or his interests, or his will to power.
Remarkably enough, these great eliminators of myth as illusion
may equally have attested the ineluctability of myth when they
came to remythicize their own thinking. Freud himself candidly
acknowledged formulating a mythology of the instincts and
constructed a compelling myth of a world presided over by
pre-Socratic divinities like *eros, thanatos,* and *ananke.* Diony-
sus and Apollo took on new life in Nietzsche's imagination, and
the grand finale of Marx's view of history and human society
has more than a passing resemblance to biblical prophecy and
apocalyptic. Nevertheless, they belong to the unmaskers of
myth and where they mythologize, they like Plato, construct
"rational" myths to indicate structures of reality not in themselves inherently mythical.

The more affirmative attitude toward myth is represented
in modern times by theologians like Rudolf Bultmann, phe-
nomenologists of religion like Paul Ricoeur, Mircea Eliade, or

Rudolf Otto, philosophers like Susanne Langer, or Ernst Cassirer, psychoanalysts of the Jungian persuasion, anthropologists like Lévi-Strauss, or literary critics like Northrop Frye.
With all their differences, these scholars and thinkers view
myth as not simply inevitable but somehow indispensable.
Myth may be the language of feelings, the expression of the
deepest layers of the psyche, the natural vehicle for man's
apprehension of the transcendent. It is not the realm of truth in
any simple sense of the term, but the realm of meanings, relations, values or, as Jaspers put it, "an inexhaustible cipher."

Platonism's distinctions between kinds of myth were also
perpetuated in the contrast drawn over many centuries between classical mythology and Christian religious revelation—
which looked quite mythical to pagan critics like Celsus. From
a secular standpoint this distinction was between "canonical"
and "apocryphal" myth.[17] Christian poets, like Milton, who
used both the classics and the Bible for their allusions obviously did not place the two bodies of myth on the same plane,
although a Christian poet need not have been hostile to classical myth and could find a place for it in the Christian scheme
of things through either a typological mode of interpretation or
a more abstract mode of interpretation usually philosophical
and neoplatonic.[18]

The Christian poet understood classical myth as a kind of
pagan *praeparatio evangelica* where some of the gods and their
acts might be construed as types forshadowing the historical
Christian revelation. Or the techniques of moral and philosophical allegory might permit an acceptable assimilation of the
tales of the "old religion." Of course, to the modern student of
literature, such a distinction between bodies of myth is nuga-
tory. Although a believing reader might accord his preferred
myth a special status in his religious life, he will probably,
reading Milton or Dante, experience all the mythical material of
the poems in the autonomous sphere of literary culture. Both
sacred and profane myths will yield those meanings peculiar to
literature. After all, everyone, even the theologian, has been
profoundly affected by Schleiermacher's cancellation of the
distinction between *hermeneutica sacra* and *hermeneutica profana*. The human mind and its acts of understanding are really

everywhere the same. Even the Bible does not escape being a book, and even the theologian has to read it as a book and confront the same sort of problems that confront the classical scholar or historian.

We may take Freud to be our last great interpreter of myth, as Plato was our first. Whatever the profound differences which separate them—and they are profound—both Plato and Freud are concerned to reveal the moral unworthiness of much of the received and normative mythological tradition, to deny any final metaphysical reality to all or most of its assumptions about the world, to discover the kind of truth that myth may in fact contain, and to make their own mythic structures more consonant with reality than those available in the surrounding culture.

The Freudian view belongs more to the tradition of elimination than conservation of the mythical even if Freud was prepared to remythicize his thinking when necessary. The myth has its roots in history, to be sure, but it is the history of the individual, projected onto a cosmic plane and shaped by the wishes and fears universally experienced by mankind in the developmental process. Various psychoanalytical views of myth and symbolism are current, but the essential view of the orthodox Freudian rests on a radical distinction between the symbolic process and the metaphorical process. True symbolism is always a disguise and emerges from the need to mask and give indirect expression to unconscious and forbidden wishes and drives. The grammar of myth and symbol, like the grammar of dreams, is that of the "language" of the primary process, the archaic language of the dream world whose syntax involves masking devices such as condensation, displacement, symbolization, a language which is in the service of the pleasure principle. The symbol for Freud is an indirect and figurative expression of an unconscious idea, conflict, or wish. It is essentially a substitute, and shares with jokes, slips of the tongue, and symptoms the function of standing for an unconscious content. It thus both expresses and conceals something which is quite capable in principle of being stated in rational terms. Moreover, there is for Freud a remarkable constancy between what is symbolized and its representation, a constancy to be found not only in a particular person but in myths, religions, and languages of all times and places. The range of symbols disclosed by psychoanalysis is quite wide, but the realities symbolized relatively few: parts of the body, especially the sexual organs, parents, birth, death. Once the patient overcomes his repression and consciously accepts the hitherto forbidden wish, he loses the need to symbolize and so disguise it. That is to say, he loses his "symptoms."

The metaphorical process, sometimes confused with the symbolic process even by some psychoanalysts, is entirely in the realm of consciousness. This process posits resemblances between realities, transferring analogous properties from one term to another, creating an expanding semantic field. For example, from the notion of the flow of water we pass to expressions like the flow of time or the stream of consciousness. The metaphorical process is thus epigenetic; new meanings are created through it, and those meanings originate in and remain in the realm of conscious, rational thought. The metaphorical process does not, in essence, find its meanings in the unconscious. A particular metaphor or figure may acquire unconscious significance for an individual but, unlike true symbolism, it does not emerge from the need to both express and hide another, unconscious meaning. The Freudian theory is abundantly clear, and it is puzzling to find psychoanalytic interpretations of art or literature confounding the metaphorical and symbolic processes.[19]

In essential respects Freud's great work is a system of hermeneutics, a universal system of interpretation—and Paul Ricoeur so views it. But in the narrower sense of interpretation, Freud has left us one book, *Moses and Monotheism,* in which he tried his hand at interpreting the most interpreted book in the world. Certainly, his work is not a contribution to ancient history or biblical scholarship, and I doubt that there are any scholars in the field who find his book on Moses and the origins of monotheism convincing. Nevertheless, the book contains a good deal of brilliant psychological analysis, and we might say, "se non è vero, è ben trovato," which might be freely translated as: if the work is not true it is nevertheless a happy invention.

A short passage in *Moses and Monotheism* contains the most penetrating of Freud's observations on interpretation and is surely valid for any reader of the Bible and of other mythological and religious texts.

The text, however, as we find it today tells us enough about its own history. Two distinct forces, diametrically opposed to each other, have left their traces on it. On the one hand, certain transformations got to work on it, falsifying the text in accord with secret tendencies, maiming and extending it until it was turned into its opposite. On the other hand, an indulgent piety reigned over it, anxious to keep everything as it stood, indifferent to whether the details fitted together or nullified one another. Thus almost everywhere there can be found striking omissions, disturbing repetitions, palpable contradictions, signs of things the communication of which was never intended. The distortion of a text is not unlike a murder. The difficulty lies not in the execution of the deed but in the doing away with the traces. One could wish to give the word "distortion" the double meaning to which it has a right, although it is no longer used in this sense. It should mean not only "to change the appearance of," but also "to wrench apart," "to put in another place." That is why in so many textual distortions we may count on finding the suppressed and abnegated material hidden away somewhere though in an altered shape and torn out of its original connection. Only it is not always easy to recognize it.[20]

In a manner parallel to that of Kaufmann, cited earlier, Freud sees the essential contradictions of the biblical text as the resolution of two "vectors" working in opposing directions. Where Kaufmann sees contradiction as emerging from the clash between the utter absoluteness of the divine will and his imputed moral nature, Freud sees the clash of the conservative tendency of traditional piety with the tendency to repress the moral evils, the guilty secrets, which tradition conserved from an ordinary past and imputed to divine agency.

Freud's exegetical methods are more, of course, than methods applied to a text—whether the text be a printed one or the "text" the patient provides in his associations and dreams. His exegesis is also a *praxis,* the application of reason to the problems of existence, the delineation of the structures of reality against the distortions of illusion. Although Freud was never sanguine about happiness, offering only to replace neurotic misery with ordinary mundane unhappiness, it is nevertheless fair to say that the final thrust of his exegesis, if it will not procure that fulfillment of childhood wishes most people take for happiness, might well provide an outcome consonant with the Greek view of happiness as the outcome of doing something specifically human surpassingly well.

Interpretation,
Humanistic Culture,
and Cultural Change

THE PREVIOUS ESSAYS in this book have dealt with situations in which interpretation is a vital activity, with style itself as a primary mode of interpretation, and with specific examples in allegory and myth of the vicissitudes of the interpretive activity. In this essay I will view interpretation from a quite different standpoint. I will attempt to clarify the role of interpretation in culture by drawing a protracted parallel between biological and cultural change and then pass to the situation of interpreters of humanistic texts in modern Western societies. Rapidity of change in modern technological societies has made continuity with the past more necessary, while certain structural cleavages in modern industrial society have made the task of interpretation as a generally necessary activity more difficult. I can offer no remedies, but perhaps I can offer a slightly different view of the problem than the reader has yet encountered.

Interpretation may be provisionally described as that activity which makes culturally significant texts intelligible. Culturally significant texts are those which are generally agreed to be worth preserving for understanding. Precisely because they require interpretation, we know their meaning and significance have become more or less problematic. What I have to say about interpretation, its occasions, and its problems, applies in some measure to sacred texts, legal texts such as the Constitution of the United States, and even to the "text" of a symphony or, figuratively, a painting. My concern will be with

95

texts of a literary and humanistic character, but I would like the reader to be aware of this larger and more comprehensive meaning of interpretation.

My first observation is that interpretive activity is mediatory. All acts of interpretation, without exception, bridge some distance which has arisen between an "invariant" text and its significance, or between a system of "fixed" signs and symbols and a diminution in its immediate intelligibility. From this point of view, we may say that the occasion of interpretation arises when we become aware that the text has undergone a kind of entropy of meaning and significance. We perceive a degree of disorder, a loss of meaning, and, as in the physical sphere, we are required to work to restore an original state of greater order and intelligibility. What I have called entropy, using a physical figure of speech, may be more conventionally described as that "distance" historical and cultural change inevitably interposes between us and the records of the past, historical, literary, or artistic.

This preliminary definition does not answer two crucial questions: who decides which texts are valuable and which are not? This is the question of what we might call cultural canon formation, the process by which some of the many cultural artifacts and texts are selected for preservation, while others are allowed to disappear. The second unanswered question is: what criteria are there for validity in interpretation? Both of these questions are related, for if we preserve Shakespeare, we do so because we take our judgments concerning his value as valid.

I do not propose to try to answer these questions head on. It is not possible to give any direct, simple, unqualified answer to them. The history of the interpretation of so important a book as the Bible would show that criteria of validity are subject to extraordinary changes, while the history of fluctuations in taste would show that our contemporary canon of "greats" might have been other than it is. These facts need not cast us adrift on the seas of historical relativism, but they do indicate that we might clarify these problems if we approach them obliquely rather than directly. More specifically, we need to understand what kind of social purposes texts have served and what kind of cultural situations create a demand for exegesis. Faithful to my oblique approach, I will begin with a short detour and consider some of the resemblances and contrasts between biological and cultural evolution. In this way, we may shed some light on the mediatory function of interpretation.

Let me first clarify my terminology. I will use the terms "literature" and "literary culture" as almost synonymous with "the humanities" or "humanistic culture." It is customary to say that the writings of a philosopher like Plato are literature, while the writings of a Spinoza or Kant are not. There is an obvious truth to this kind of distinction. It is, however, too reminiscent of the distinction which used to be drawn between "belles lettres" and a lot of magnificent and important writing which was somehow not "belle." I would prefer to open up the term literature to all of those works, historical, philosophical, religious, as well as "poetic," which possess some legitimate claim to moral, imaginative, and intellectual authority, in whatever proportions these qualities may occur in a given instance. Both autumn and Spinoza have their beauties.

Analogies can be drawn between literature so defined and the arts of painting, sculpture, and architecture, and I will have the occasion to include artists among observations about literature. While my definition is thus very wide, I do exclude much that is purely entertainment, propaganda, or journalism.

I will have occasion to discuss the role of literature at different times in history and I would remind the reader that literature, even the greatest literature, was not to be found only in a written text, nor was its dissemination wholly dependent on a written text. Much of the great literature of the world was available to illiterate or semiliterate peoples through recitation, dramatic presentation where appropriate, or through the sermon and oration. Printing, the inexpensive book, and widespread literacy have profoundly changed the character of the audience for literature as well as the character of literature itself. It is impossible to imagine that the poems of Wallace Stevens or the prose of Henry James, however tuned by the rhythms of speech, could ever be read to an audience, literate or illiterate, and be readily understood.

Homer, the Bible, the *Chanson de Roland,* Greek and

Elizabethan drama reached great audiences who would never have been able to read a text at all. Such works were, in a way, self-interpreting at one time in their history. A literature meant to be heard cannot allow itself the intellectual and aesthetic complexities in its surface manifestation that a literature meant to be read can permit itself. We may doubt that the barely literate reader of the Bible really understood it as he should, but we cannot doubt that there was a level of the work which he did grasp, which shaped his will, his imagination, and his powers of expression. So, too, even for the illiterate hearer of the biblical text. Today we witness a curious paradox: a functional literacy has never been more widely diffused, while the technology of the printed, inexpensive book allows the author to be as difficult as he needs to be. The greatest of modern literature is difficult and demanding but, while potentially available to the many, is read by the few.

What I have to say about the different kinds of literary and humanistic elites and the principles of interpretation they call forth will be somewhat clearer if my reader sets aside the customary assumptions he brings to his understanding of how literature is appropriated and reflects upon a past when those assumptions did not apply.

If we take the biblical "three-score and ten," the human life span, as our unit of temporal measure, then biological evolution is enormously slow while cultural evolution is tremendously rapid. Even a relatively static culture changes with great rapidity when measured against the aeons of geological and biological time. Against the cosmic clock, the present and past cultural diversity of the world has all occurred in an instant. But much of man's speculations about himself, his nature and his destiny, have been determined by his perception of the natural world as stable. Its species appear to remain constant, while the historical world is rich in change, hybrids, and transformations. It is important for us to remember that this contrast is only relatively true, that man is just as much a part of the course of biological evolution as all other organisms, however little he may perceive it, and that culture finally serves the biological purpose of adapting man to his environment and fostering the survival of the species. At least, we can guardedly assume that this is what culture is supposed to do, aware as we are of the present possibilities for self-extinction or technological change so rapid that we cannot quite keep up with its sometimes unpredictable or destructive consequences.

The mechanism of biological evolution is clearly understood: natural selection works on the random variation of species to shape the transformations of living matter. The ultimate source of genetic novelty is mutation, a change in the molecules carrying the genetic information which guides the course of the individual's development and makes him both an individual and a member of a particular species. But there is immense variety in the manifestations of even a single species, variety brought about through that recombination and reassortment of existent genes which takes place in the sexual process. Even with the lowest possible rate of mutation, of genetic novelty, there is still plenty of variety in the gene pool of an interbreeding population for natural selection to work on. Only a part of the genetic potential of any species is manifested at one time, and we all carry genes whose expression, for good or ill, is reserved for our descendants. The appearance of a mutation, or the expression of a new variety, forever changes the biological texture of the world. Extinct species will never return any more than extinct individuals.

All living things are interrelated in so many vital and complex ways that they may be said to constitute virtually a single super-organism. This interdependence of organisms means that each biological change in some small measure changes the whole, so that the course of biological evolution is irreversible. Cultural evolution, on the other hand, would appear to be reversible in a very significant way. Great civilizations have declined and been replaced with populations living much like the primitive predecessors of the civilization whose ruins they inhabit. Although we have hitherto witnessed only a shift in the centers of civilization and not its global extinction, it does not seem possible to say that such a total extinction, under circumstances short of the total annihilation of the race, might not occur. In any event, the dynamics of cultural change, whether we deal with instances we think of as progressive or retrogressive, is by no means clearly understood. It even seems too difficult to find any wide agreement on what, in detail, cultural progress or decay might be. Biological change can be viewed with an objectivity which seems to be impossible, and may not even be desirable, when we come to consider cultural and historical life. The idea of indefinite progress of the human race has revealed itself as so ambiguous that there is scarcely a cultural or technological innovation which will not be both hailed and deplored, with powerful arguments on either side of the judgment.

Thus, although the idea of progress has long been banished from the sphere of biological evolution, students of cultural evolution seem unable to do without some covert if not overt form of it. In the final analysis this is so because we do not seem to be able to ask of the human race that it merely survive, although that is the indispensable requirement of any of the many possible arrangements for conducting human affairs. The anthropologist may view Patagonian fire worshippers or Australian aborigines with that detachment suitable to a scientist, but the instant he thinks of that alien culture in relation to his own or another, he must suppress the inevitable question of whether one arrangement may not be better than another, even if a given phenomenon must be understood in light of the fact that a culture is all of a piece. The point is that the question does arise and the scientist, *qua* scientist, has to suppress it. Kant tells us that the great achievement of the enlightenment could be expressed in the motto *sapere aude,* "Dare to know," and this must be the guide of the scientific investigator of human as well as natural phenomena. But this standpoint, as Kant well knew, is that of pure reason and excludes much of great concern. He did after all, write the *Critique of Practical Reason* and the *Critique of Judgment* wherein all that pure reason threw out the window came marching in through the door for consideration.

Yet it may be profitable for us to view cultural evolution in the light of biological evolution in spite of the difficulties. We do not very often ask of a specific phenomenon in the higher cultures what its adaptational function or survival value might be. To dare to know is to strip illusion from the world in the name of reason, but one may well ask whether some illusions serve some vital function, or are adaptive to reality itself. The idea of vitally necessary fiction, the role of a kind of "untruth" in human life, is at least as old as Plato, where it appears as political necessity, but Darwin and Freud may permit us to view necessary fictions, however defined, in biological terms. It is unfortunate that the first modern cultural Darwinism was Spencerian. In retrospect, it seems almost unbelievably simplistic and cruel and involved little more than looking for the cultural counterpart of the "struggle for existence" or the "survival of the fittest." Such formulae did not even give a good account of biological evolution, much less of cultural evolution. The upshot of social Darwinism was the remarkable discovery that the rich were far better fitted to survive than the poor. Indeed, that was the very reason they were rich.

More recently, geneticists have entered the field of cultural biologism but with disappointing results. At considerable length, it is affirmed that cultural progress is a result of the genetic constitution of those making it, with no precise explanation of how we get from one to the other. If fifth-century Athens or fifteenth-century Florence was crammed with genius, there must have been some genetic factors which made that possible. Indeed there must, but the interesting questions are how and in what degree genetic factors account for cultural achievement and why cultural declines can occur so precipitously when the genetic constitution of the people cannot possibly have changed very much in the interval. Both Spencer and the geneticists err in the attempt to reduce the rapid cultural process of change to the millenial biological one.[1]

There are, however, correspondences between cultural evolution and biological evolution even if we cannot reduce the one to the other, and we may ask of cultural innovations some of the same questions we ask of biological innovations. We may define man's power to symbolize as the principle of both cultural stability and cultural innovation, for it shares two essential characteristics of the genetic system. The system of heredity, while extraordinarily stable from generation to generation, slowly permits the creation of genetic novelties as well as the continual reassortment and recombination of both old and new genetic information. Through the symbolic systems of art, science, magic, religion, and myth, man not only manipulates himself and his environment, but renders culture both stable enough to be inherited and capable of adaptational change. As we shall see, adaptational change in the cultural sphere is the work of interpretation, the often but not always deliberate act by which old meanings are modified to deal with new situations.

That this comparison is not purely extrinsic becomes clear when we observe the use of concepts from information and communication theory to describe the functions of the genetic molecule DNA. In nature and in culture the common process is the transmission of information. The fertilized egg does not contain the miniature adult but the instruction, coded in a giant molecule, for making the adult through a long and complex process of development. The newborn baby, having just entered the cultural realm, must be "informed" to recreate and give continuity to the culture of his parents. The biological and cultural legacy of the ancestors both must be remade, manifested anew, in each generation.

If variability in the biological realm occurs through mutation and recombination of genes, variability in the cultural sphere comes about through the metaphorical process, the capacity of the human mind through the resources of language to discern resemblances and signify something through an analogical relation with something old. It is, moreover, what we often discern as the ambiguity of language that permits meanings to be transformed by extending them from one event to another, whether new or old, which resembles it. It is precisely this ambiguity or semantic variability which opens the way to new meanings, to new cultural variations.

There is also a kind of analogue to natural selection which operates on semantic variations, a kind of selective pressure eliminating meanings from that common pool of meanings that contains all that we conserve from the past. Deliberately or not, humanity continually tests its beliefs, hypotheses, and opinions, not always for their rationality by any means, but surely always in terms of some sense, however vague, of their adaptational value. The error of some rationalists has been to assume that if a structure of meaning or belief is literally "untrue," it is therefore of no value or serves no vital purpose. The result is to render vast areas of human experience and behavior unintelligible. The realm of meaning is not identical by any means with the realm of verifiable propositions, and the discovery of fresh meanings and relations in the welter of experience may well require, in the first instance, the use of our poetic and myth making powers.[2]

It has been thought possible, and may even be illuminating, to view culture in its totality as a vast and complex symptomatic fiction whose function is defensive, a mere curb on instinct. From this point of view, all of culture may appear as both irrational and vitally necessary at the same time. Freud valued the rational component of culture much too highly to view it in this light and was content to accept the discomforts of civilization for reason's incalculable benefits. Some modern radicalizers of psychoanalytic theory will not stop where Freud stopped, however, and prophecy a world in which culture, as we know it anyway, will have disappeared to be replaced with a millenium of instinctual gratification and harmony. They thus confer on the emotional life the properties which we have long thought were conferred by reason working in harmony with the emotions.

But the avenging furies in Aeschylus do not disappear. They are persuaded to change into the Eumenides, in which transformation their destructive energies become creative and are placed in the service of life and rational order. Plato's Demiurge does not coerce the preexistent chaos to become cosmos, but gradually imposes rational order on the swirling, shapeless primeval substrate. The vital energy of the nonrational, emotional, biological component of existence is not, in the final analysis, the mere antithesis of reason. A disembodied rationality may be appropriate to the life hereafter but has no place in this one. Spinoza, whom Nietzsche called the wisest of sages, tells us that the gift of reason is joy, *gaudium,* and that we are made to possess it.

Our models for historical-cultural change and romantic cultural biologism are various, but the great classic models, except for social Darwinism, are all essentially pre-Darwinian insofar as their regulatory principles are teleological. The moment the cultural historian or the philosopher of history finds progression in some grand historical design or, indeed, if he finds a grand design at all, he is inevitably within the teleological sphere if not a theological one. Modern biologists, to be sure, severely exclude any form of metaphysical teleology from the theory of biological evolution. If they speak of purposes they do not imply nature realizes purposes in any way that human beings realize purposes. To say that the purpose of the heart is to pump blood does not imply anything metaphysical. Nor does any taxonomic arrangement of organisms along a hierarchy of complexity imply a corresponding hierarchy of value. It is possible to say that the amoeba is somewhat simpler than a tiger, but the amoeba we perceive through the microscope is the product of as long an evolutionary process— longer, in fact—as the tiger that stalks its prey in the jungle. As far as we can tell, both effectively perform all the indispensable functions of living and fit quite effectively into their respective environmental niches.

Despite Darwin, a good many of the older generation of biologists were pleased to view evolution as the history of the climb of life from simple creatures living in primeval ooze, up the great cosmic ladder, to man standing at its apex. Such a scheme of things seemed consonant with the equally pleasing notion of a Creator who accomplished some grand, intelligible plan of things. But the model of biological evolution is much more like a bush than a ladder. The various phyla are viewed as radiating outward from a common root in many possible directions, with branches and twigs of widely differing size and shape. Indeed, to use Darwin's figure in another context, the evolutionary landscape is a "tangled bank" and not a cosmic ladder.

The interpretation of historical and cultural change more often than not has eluded this process of demythologizing. It is surprising how pervasive the influence of Hegel, Marx, Comte, Spengler, or Toynbee still is in contemporary thought on the subject. There may be some understandable reasons for this, and we should glance, however briefly, at the views of these thinkers before rejecting them out of hand.

Hegel apparently could not have cared less about natural

science, and his attempt to deduce the categories of nature is a colossal failure. He is more interesting in what he has to say about the history of thought, where he discerned the heart beat of all history. The dynamism of cultural change, in Hegel's point of view, is nothing less than the dynamism of thought itself, reason moving from one position to another dialectically and ending with bringing to consciousness the totality of what is thinkable. Marx's dialectical materialism purported to make Hegel's absolute stand on its feet instead of its head, and he found the mainspring of cultural change in the successive changes of the organization of economic life and those ideological transformations which accompany them. For Comte, the heart of change was the laboratory: science progresses and finally overtakes and supplants its religious and metaphysical forerunners. Spengler and Toynbee, in somewhat differing ways, adapt an organismic analogy to explain historical change. Each civilization progresses from birth through maturity to senescence and death. Toynbee, in contrast to Spengler, views each civilization or higher culture as depositing a world religion on the sands of time, a religious world view to be taken up by the civilization which succeeds it. Spengler's civilizations do not appear to make such generous legacies before they vanish from our eyes.

Such large schemes of explanation survive because we have not replaced them, to be sure, but they are also stimulating to the imagination and serve to bring to our attention relations between cultural phenomena that we might not have otherwise noticed. They also serve temporarily to assure us that historical life is not as confused and cluttered as it sometimes appears to be, that one pattern or other is discernible in all that buzz. They may also, unfortunately, persuade us that we know far more about the order of things than we in fact do. Such systems are, in fact, more or less secularized theodicies which attempt to justify God's ways to man, often leaving him out, however, and unable therefore to assure us that someone knows what it is all about even if we mere humans are afforded only a mouse-view of the whole.

There are other, perhaps more important reasons why such overarching systems cannot attain any kind of general assent. The authors of the classic philosophies of history and cultural change advance very obscure criteria for deciding how, concretely, we may determine whether we are progressing or decaying. Is the decline of traditional religions a sign of progress or decay? Is the advance of science and its attendant technologies really a sure sign of progress? To ask such questions is to realize that large generalizations about progress, however described, are really disguised theological propositions and demand acts of faith as wholehearted as those of devout believers in the God of revelation.

Moreover, there is a sense in which it is true that historical evolution does not leave a static fossil record behind it, but that historical fossils are still alive. Science does not replace magic. It exists side by side with it. Reason does not replace superstition. Superstitions abound at no great distance from centers of scientific and scholarly inquiry. Indeed, voices are now being raised which envision a future so overwhelmed by population growth, pressure on natural resources, and the spread of nuclear weapons that science, technology, and free societies may be banished from the earth as luxuries which the human race can no longer afford.

Future generations may well be reluctant Arcadians instead of the energetic Utopians we have often been and look back nostalgically on a golden age which they have forever lost. This "scenario" sees a static, coercive, mythical-religious society inevitable in the future. It is the price we must pay for survival. Dystopia thus appears on the horizon as a society where survival demands a minimum of individual change and a maximum of disciplined, specialized coordination. Nature has evolved similar societies before. They exist before our eyes in beehives and anthills. There, behavior is under strict chemical control, and biological functions are rigidly distributed so that individual existence is totally subordinated to the existence of the whole. I present this simply as a frivolously modernized Aesopian fable, but it is not without its moral either.[3]

In the light of this imaginative possibility, however remote, it is difficult to pray at the shrine of Comte, Hegel, and the rest. The dominion of science, or religion, or philosophy will not usher in the millenium. It is not even possible to de-

plore the dominion of technology unequivocally, if only because the hopes of millions of people in Asia, Africa, and Latin
America rest on obtaining for themselves precisely those conditions of material progress which some tender souls among our
contemporaries so utterly despise. Their lives are too unmiti-
gatedly harsh for them to be willing to feed the pastoral fantasies of Western European and American tourists. They feel
they have a right—and who can deny it to them?—to the
benefits of technological progress. They are more than willing
to assume the risks, even though they may be greater than
those we have incurred, for the massive and rapid superimposi-
tion of technology on simpler societies creates even more extreme cultural conflict than we have experienced. We may view
that cost as too high, but it is clear that the so-called underde-
veloped peoples do not.

In contrast to all this, the biological landscape seems simpler. We do not have to ask all the complex questions which
inevitably concern us when we deal with specifically human
problems, at least not with the same urgency or inevitability
and certainly not with a view to diagnosing the course of biological evolution. Yet we are animals, however different from
the other species we think we are, and we may return to the
biological sphere of things and depart instructed. "Speak to the
earth and it shall teach thee," says one of his comforters to
Job, and if what Job learned was to contemplate creation and
learn the impossibility of all theodicies, there may be a valuable
lesson for us in trying to do the same, even without benefit of a
magisterial voice from the whirlwind to instruct us.

Biological evolution, as we have seen, rests on an intricate
balance between a principle of invariance, the stability from
generation to generation of existent structures of a species, and
variation, the gradual modification of species over a long period
of time. The source of genetic novelties, of new genes, is ultimately mutation. DNA, the giant informational macro-molecule
in which the instructions for development of the individual are
stored, must change if a genetic novelty is to appear in the
world. By far, however, most of the variation we discern at any
time in a particular species is not the result of mutation but of
the recombination and reassortment of genes through the sex-

ual process. It is that process which gives differential expression to the totality of genes in the gene pool of species. The existent gene pool of the human race without any genetic changes at all could still express enormous variety, only a small part of which is actualized at any definite time.

Over a short time, the essential structure of a species is astonishingly stable, so much so that it took an enormous intellectual effort over several generations to establish incontrovertibly the fact of biological evolution. Only a trained intelligence working with particular materials can see evolution at work. Yet all species we know slowly and gradually do change. And the gradualness of the change is most important. Abrupt changes, whether due to alteration of the genetic material or to the manifest expression of a gene lying in the existent complex, are rarely if ever salutary. If an organism is not as immutable as a fine watch, it is not as plastic as sculptor's clay. The changes which take place in a species normally are quite small, and most of them seem to confer no obvious immediate advantage or disadvantage to the individual. It is only over long periods and changing conditions that natural selection acts, through favoring some varieties over another, to create new species.

The point of interest here is that the rate of evolutionary change is gradual and that its fluctuations occur within relatively narrow limits. A species must preserve an enormous amount of continuity with its past if it is to change and still survive. Biological structures cannot simply be dismantled and immediately replaced with different substitutes. What this may imply for cultural change is obvious if not susceptible of precise formulation.

A remarkable feature of the history of biological evolution which throws stronger light on cultural evolution is the fact that similar structures, even structures as complex as eyes, have arisen quite independently in the course of evolution to perform the same function. Apparently, living matter invented the eye more than once in its long history. The streamlined body form of quite unrelated creatures of the sea, the eyes of the octopus and the eyes of man, however similar, appear to have had no common ancestor. The shaping power of natural selection working on the potentialities of living matter in its protean variation produced them independently. But evolution is not only innovative. It is also conservative and economical. The anterior forelimbs of various mammals, for example, did evolve from a common ancestral character, but sometimes became adapted to quite different functions. The flippers of the whale derive from the limbs of an animal originally able to move about on land, but now serve the purposes of an animal confined to water. These two features of evolution, the one innovative, the other conservative, are related respectively to the principle of biological analogy and the principle of biological homology.[4]

If similar features arise independently of one another in different evolutionary lines, we have an instance of analogy. If the same feature becomes modified to perform a different function, we have an instance of homology. The one represents the innovative character of evolution and the other its traditional character. However much analogous structures resemble each other, they essentially are new creations. Homologous structures are more like hand-me-downs, old materials still worthy of use with a little tailoring here and there.

Like biological change, cultural change is both conservative and innovative. Since any culture serves the function of preserving the species, it is necessary that a culture be inheritable if we are to survive. And if a culture be inherited, it must possess a large measure of invariance. Our arrangements for work, marriage, childrearing must be largely invariant from generation to generation. Obviously, stability of such arrangements does not mean immutability. A culture whose institutions cannot adapt to change cannot survive the continually changing circumstances under which men must live. Of course, gross cultural changes may produce some monstrous formations, quite as unviable as those at times produced in nature by excessive rapidity of change. It is well to bear in mind that no revolution, however radical its premises, ever succeeded which did not come to terms with and preserve powerful elements of continuity with its prerevolutionary past.

Each such act of preservation involved some act of reinterpretation of that past in order to preserve it. Turning a church into a museum is one way of preserving it after all and—who knows?—people may again stop to pray in it. Interpretation may also make it clear that if all the citizens of a state are absolutely equal in principle, some may well be more equal than others in practice. Orwell's sardonic observations of the fate of the egalitarian principle should not deflect us from reflecting on the possibility that even the most relentlessly egalitarian ideology may have to make room for differentiation of power and privilege in practice. The disappointment of utopian revolutionaries with the outcome of their plans may have less to do with betrayals, or human depravity, or cultural lag than with the inevitable consequences of too sharp a break with the necessarily invariant aspects of culture. Cultural and social structures serve adaptive functions. They arise to serve vital human needs however irrational, confining, or conventional they may appear to the utopian eye. It is of the greatest importance that we determine those purposes before we dismantle such structures, for the purposes will be served whether we will or no.

Peaceful cultural change, cultural evolution rather than cultural revolution, validates itself through interpretive acts, for only interpretation can mediate between the past and the present laden with the future. Insofar as cultures innovate, they do so without immediately or totally destroying existing structures. Similar myths, techniques, practices arise in widely separated cultures apparently quite independently of one another and gradually assimilate and replace their predecessors. We may think of such cultural innovations, independently generated, as the cultural equivalent of biological analogies.

But the changes which interpretation validates are really "homologizing" changes. Contrary to the scriptural injunction, the interpreter pours new wine into old bottles and without necessarily spoiling the wine. Our culture abounds with old structures given fresh meanings and brought into a fresh functional relationship to the world. What I am describing has many commonplace manifestations. The legal process is certainly one instance of the homologizing process, wherein an old law, or an old constitution, remains invariant while it acquires fresh meanings and applications. The evolution of religion also shows this process at work. Human sacrifice gives way to animal sacrifice which in turn gives way to symbolic sacrifice. It is a long distance from Jephtha's sacrifice of his daughter to giving up meat for Lent, but there is continuity in the process by which we get from one act, bloody and barbarous, to another much more consonant with civilized life.

We need not assume that everything preserved in a culture is necessarily useful or functional, any more than we can assume all biological characteristics that are conserved are absolutely necessary. A trait or characteristic may be preserved because it is connected with something that is functionally vital, but both culture and nature give ample evidence of vestigial organs. There are some cultural counterparts of the vermiform appendix, a vestigial organ now useless, which may even have given us trouble and which serves at best only to remind us of an archaic past. The stream of life and the stream of human culture both carry some flotsom and jetsam along the tides of change and neither the ingenuity of man or nature can homologize every detail. It is sufficient if the ensemble works.

Only recently have we begun to escape from a long and powerful tradition of aesthetic and teleological exaltation over the works of nature. The eye was recurrently discussed as the symbol of nature and the perfect craftsman. In this organ, it seemed, metaphysical teleology may be vindicated. It is no accident that Lucretius, in his attack on such notions, is constrained to give an explicit account of the eye as the product of a chance concentration of atoms falling and swerving in the void.

Much later and much more prosaically than Lucretius, Helmholtz remarked—signalizing a major break with the traditional rhetoric of teleological rapture—that if his lens maker had sent him an eye to use as an instrument in his laboratory, he would have returned it with precise suggestions for major improvements. Galen's massive systematization of the aesthetic-teleological approach to nature, so characteristic of Greek thought, was a long time dying and survived well into modern times.

The historian of culture may usefully exorcise the remaining ghosts of teleological thinking and aesthetic contemplation from his view of things if he is to recover a human sympathy for the more remote and alien aspects of the past. He may then find a useful understanding of much that had previously struck him as merely irrational, inefficient, or dated. Every cultural fossil once had a vital part to perform in the economy of human life, and cultural fossils, unlike biological ones, may in altered circumstances live again.

The resemblances and contrasts I have tried to draw between biological and cultural evolution, the parallels between biological adaptation and the art of interpretation, must not be pressed too far. It is useful, however, to press them a little, because of those enormously powerful traditions in our own culture that lead us to make excessively sharp divisions between man and nature, nature and culture, or, on another level, between the world of natural science as the world of fact and the world of historical understanding as the world of value. A metaphysical dualism which goes back as far as Plato still exerts its influence, often in a Cartesian transformation, in our habitual way of drawing distinctions between mind and body, appearance and reality, being and becoming. Ethical monotheism and its secularized derivatives, among which we can locate contemporary existentialism, separates man from nature in religious and/or moral terms. Man and man alone is made in the image of God, or man and man alone possesses a unique way of being in the world. When those who hold such points of view philosophize about nature, if they do so at all, they are likely to view it as symbolic of a transcendant reality or as the mindless, dead, cosmic backdrop for the inexplicable appearance of a problematic human consciousness.

Ironically, modern science has encouraged this kind of dualism. It emerged in the seventeenth century armed with the promise of Baconian utilitarianism, and while it conserved the tradition that knowledge was worth having for its own sake, it nevertheless promised to give mankind that dominion over nature which God had offered to Adam and Eve and which their descendants had long expected in vain.

Bacon's *Great Instauration*—his plan for the reformation of all learning and the completion of acquiring that kind of learning which gives us dominion over nature—is divided into six parts, each a great work that mankind must accomplish in the execution of the plan. The seventh part of the great scheme is an endless sabbath of rest in the possession of that dominion. The resemblance of this scene to the opening chapter of Genesis is not fortuitous.

These powerful intellectual and moral traditions are surely not without their measure of truth, but they have widely spread the conviction that nature is merely the presupposition of culture, a foundation for the work of culture which is somehow discontinuous with its natural substrate. Maintained without great qualifications, this view has become dangerously obsolete. The current environmental crisis, the growing interest in ecology and ethology, our concern over the social implications of new biological and medical technologies are all signs of a growing awareness, forced upon us by events, that human life in all of its manifestations is inextricably bound to the laws of nature in ways far more intricate than we were aware of. We should not underestimate the significance of this phenomenon. It is far more than a matter of recycling wastes, or getting enough gasoline, or cutting down on pollution. More than our physical well-being is at stake. Our moral being and our very sanity depend on discerning the limits of what we can do and of living with those limits.

We are not free to do anything we please with this planet. This simple fact is now being pressed into our awareness by new knowledge and new problems, and we are being compelled to learn that we cannot simply introduce a technological novelty merely because it is possible to do so. We must begin to weigh even the remote consequences of our actions when it may be very difficult to know precisely what those consequences may be. The most momentous cultural fact of the times is that culture has begun to affect the course of biological evolution in massive ways, and we cannot as yet foresee the full consequences of what we are doing.

The humanities have always been as much concerned with human limitations as with human possibilities. Indeed, we recognize a tragedy or a comedy precisely because they disclose the ironic, painful, or ludicrous ways in which men do confront their limitations as well as the way in which those limitations may call out human responses of immeasurable value. That so much of the great literature, art, and philosophy of the world deals with death is the most obvious sign of concern with the limiting elements of existence and of human possibilities in confronting them. So there is much in traditional humanism which has affinities with our new emergent sense of man's relation to the world.

Before the full-scale emergence of modern science and the wide diffusion of the ideology of progress, truth was thought to be the possession of past generations. Somehow, degeneration had set in sometime between the present and a past golden age of knowledge and wisdom. Every advance in knowledge seemed to be, and often was, the recovery of what man once knew that somehow had fallen into obscurity. We may well have fallen into the opposite error of thinking about the truth, at least the truly important one, is waiting for us in the future. Certainly, for us the hallmark of truth is more likely to be its novelty than its age. Hence we are impatient with proverbs, platitudes, and cliches. A student who remarked that the choruses of Greek tragedy sounded like his grandfather in the advice they gave the protagonists was not very far off the mark. It is after all true, however banal, that too many cooks spoil the soup, even if it is also true that many hands make light work. Our difficulty with the wisdom literature of the past may be less with its apparent irrelevance than with the difficulty we have in experiencing the truth in what is repeated so often. This difficulty should not prevent us from noting that a good deal of wisdom may reside in the experienced truth of a platitude.

I have strayed somewhat from our consideration of interpretation, or from "hermeneutics" as it used to be called in a more theological time. I have also not as yet been very concrete in my treatment of this subject. But circling around the subject will have accomplished its purpose if I have demonstrated the literally vital and adaptive role interpretation has played in the history of both sacred and secular exegesis. That history is filled with anomalies. Over and over again we find that biblical or classical texts, for example, are given absurd meanings, so wide of what we take to be the mark that we are at a loss to understand the exegetical motive. To begin to understand that history we must realize that at some times and places making suitable sense of a text at whatever cost in plausibility or coherence, was vitally important. The Homeric poems remained the basis of Greek education long after a changing moral consciousness found the stories immoral and unbefitting the divine nature. Allegorization, however tendentious and far from the intention of the poet, was the only way to save the text and save morality too. The ferocity of certain injunctions in the Pentateuch have rarely been acted upon in history, but the sacred scrolls occupy an honored place in any synagogue. Both Christians and Jews have frequently observed strenuous sabbath laws, but rarely has a man been stoned to death for picking up sticks on the sabbath. The choice between adaptation through interpretation or abandoning the text often appears as the choice between cultural survival or cultural extinction. In such instances, interpretation saves the necessary fiction and domesticates it.

Clearly, only texts of a sacred and normative character demand and receive such attention and intellectual effort. The literature which serves as the cultural and moral guide of a people is not only worthy of this effort; it attracts the finest minds to its service. Exegesis is always the work of an intellectual and spiritual elite, but the work of this elite in the past was performed on behalf of a people. Its excogitated meanings, directly and indirectly, reached the community as a whole. Only in modern times has interpretation become largely an activity performed by an elite for an elite, one perhaps inevitable result of the secularization of culture and the desacralization of literary and humanistic texts.

Literary and humanistic culture is today obviously if guiltily elitist. The guilt derives, perhaps, from the conviction that humanistic culture is really for all men, while theoretical physics, for example, in the nature of things finds few able to understand it, however universally significant it might be. I do not think this is necessarily true. It is, nevertheless, an opinion which is widely held and which impedes us from grasping that the truly profound cleavage in modern culture is less between the humanistic and scientific culture than between mass culture and the kind of understanding of science and the humanities which demands considerable effort to acquire. Scientists and humanists, after all, share many common values and are animated by a similar spirit. I need not dwell on the values implic-itly and explicitly conveyed by those who create and dissemi-nate mass culture.

In our historical experience, only a universally shared reli-gion and, in quite a different way, a universally shared or de-sired technology, have ever been able to claim the imaginative and intellectual commitments of a whole people, illiterates and intellectuals alike. It makes no difference that the ordinary citi-zen did not understand the first thing about that technology he revered. The medieval serf knew nothing at all about St. Thomas either. Technologist and ignorant laymen, scholastic and igno-rant serf united in their loyalty to a common culture, however differently they perceived it.

The role of the emergent secular, humanistic culture of the Renaissance may seem an exception to this generalization—many had no direct share in it—yet it had enormous effect in shaping the social, political, and aesthetic life of the times. This was true for at least two reasons which no longer obtain. The historians, writers, thinkers, and artists of the age inherited a sacred aura which learning and art had long possessed derived from a hitherto largely sacral character. This alone gave to such activities an intangible but effective authority. Even those who had no direct share in scholarly work considered it as both prestigious and legitimate. Moreover, neither specialization of learning nor of function had fragmented the coherence of the cultural leaders of the Renaissance. The intellectuals of the period often enough were themselves statesmen, courtiers, dip-lomats, or churchmen, involved with the affairs of men and inextricably commingled, for better or worse, with the wielders of power.

Thus, while it is true that an Erasmus, a More, a Machia-velli, or a Milton did not write for the multitude, their political, social, and moral concerns were common concerns, even if their views were not accepted or they failed in the practical sphere of life. They sought to define the moral and political destiny of peoples. This could be, as we know, a dangerous enterprise, more so then than now. More may have lost his head and Machiavelli suffered exile, but they certainly did not suffer the ultimate ignominy of being ignored.

The so-called revival of classical learning in the Renaissance was a renewed interest in books then understood to be both intrinsically valuable and immensely practical. The classics were viewed simultaneously as formally beautiful and as comprehensive records of the moral, intellectual and imaginative experience of the human race. They delineated, in imaginatively compelling ways, the appropriate goals and aspirations of mankind as well as the pitfalls and tragic dilemmas. They were normative books, and it was this understanding of them that gave them their quasi-sacred character. The profound differences between that society and our own have created a situation in which humanistic culture has little direct effect on the political and social life of the community as a whole.

Technological society requires an ever increasing differentiation of functions and tasks. Techniques continually proliferate and each such innovation requires training. The extraordinary degree of coordination and differentiation required to run a great city or industry shrinks the arena of individual action. If all the world can still be viewed as a stage, it is hard to find the hero amid all the extras going about their business in the great spectacle. Technology transforms the world, not only by what it does, but by what it is and the way it works. By its very mode of existence, it conveys the values of specialization, efficiency, and rationalization of procedures. It can claim the major role in changing the character of the human will by transforming human goals. It has profoundly affected the desires of mankind and raised our threshold of expectation. No educational and religious system could do more.

There are, however, signs of a general understanding that the growth of one kind of knowledge, technical knowledge, has created a need for other kinds of knowledge, the kind of knowledge of ourselves to be found in literature, philosophy, religion, and art. The dominion over nature promised by technology has often turned out to be dominion exercised by a few powerful men. Moreover, the natural world will not allow us carelessly to exploit its bounty. Our control of nature has served in the outcome to remind us that the power we need is the power to control ourselves.

I do not wish to claim that the study of the cultural legacy of the past is a sufficient condition for what used to be called wisdom. It is, I think, a necessary condition in that wisdom rests on the appropriation of what is typical and recurrent in the experience of the human race. Whitehead observed that wisdom is freedom in the presence of knowledge, not knowledge itself, or even any particular knowledge. For this reason no curriculum can guarantee to give wisdom, a fact the courts recognized when they threw out a case brought by a Columbia student against the University for failing to make him wise. If, in fact, he recognized that he was not wise, he may well have been eligible to enter the Socratic company of the seekers of wisdom who are, at least, on the right track.

Nor should wisdom be confused with what we call mental health or making a good adjustment. Nietzsche, after all, was extraordinarily wise and extraordinarily maladjusted. The distinctively modern wisdom therapy of psychoanalysis claims to free us from the tyranny of the past—and our past, individual and collective, can sometimes exert a tyrannical authority over us. But the study of the historical and humanistic legacy has the equally necessary function of freeing us from tyranny of the present. Great periods of cultural innovation were often enough inaugurated in the name of recovering some valued past, so that the way to go forward may well involve more than a casual backward glance.

Such a search for a personally effective kind of knowledge has always brought with it a heightened interest in interpretation. It is no accident that both the Renaissance and our own time are markedly ages of exegesis and interpretation. Whether the task of interpretation is the unmasking of the past or its conservation, larger and larger areas of human experience have become the subject of the most elaborate interpretive systems we have ever known. While technology has widely promoted a futuristic orientation, literary and humanistic intellectuals have never been more concerned with the uses of the past. This fact would appear to have widened the gulf between the literary elite and a technological and managerial elite.

A cultural situation in which literature is written for and by an elite is by no means entirely new. Hellenistic times saw the kind of writer who bears more resemblance to the modern writer than to his classical forerunners. Both in the hellenistic Greek world and its Roman successor, there first appeared the writer with the avowed and primary intention of charming his audience or of dazzling it with rhetorical pyrotechnics. The pastorals, the novelistic romances, the flood of epideictic orations totally divorced from any legal or political function made no further claim than this upon their audiences. The world had changed and the high aim of shaping the moral imagination of a people had been abandoned. Certainly, the mythical-religious tradition had lost its power to serve as a storehouse of meanings and values from which the writer could draw. No intellectual reposed any belief in the old stories, and the masses had long before begun to turn to religions whose common denominator was a promise of salvation. A strong tradition of high artificiality entered into later Greek literature and dominated even the greatest of Roman writers—an extraordinary verbal and rhetorical dexterity for its own sake and not for the service of some larger end. St. Augustine's attack on the powerful rhetorical tradition was finally right. The truth, particularly the truth which sets men free, has a greater claim on us and greater beauty than all the flowers of rhetoric taken together.

While the Roman intelligentsia cultivated their sensibilities, among the masses of the Roman empire profound religious transformations were taking place which would eventually give birth to new gods and a new civilization. The elite was largely ignorant or uncaring of what Yeats called that "rough beast, its hour come around at last, slouching towards Bethlehem to be born." An immense chasm had opened up between the values of the cultural and political leaders of the Empire and the great populations they ruled. Many reasons have been adduced for the decline of the ancient civilizations. Rostovtzeff, perhaps the greatest modern historian of that period, believed that the most important factor was the failure of the cultural elite to perpetuate and, more important, to disseminate the values which had once been the source of their strength. What Gibbon called the triumph of Christianity and barbarism over civilization may well have been a battle in which the losing side has lost before the battle was even joined.

As the role of literature changes with great social and cultural changes, the character of acts of interpretation changes. Texts formerly sacred are read as secular texts. Texts that instructed a people with models of conduct or goals of aspiration are read for individualistic purposes, or cultural reasons. This is by no means inappropriate if we are ever to read and learn from the literature of a past more remote than our father's generation.

The greatest works of the past are precisely those than survive beyond the situation which called them into being. They can adapt, and each successive fresh interpretation may be viewed as contributing to a series of homologizing adaptations, the old structures finding new functions and fresh uses.[5]

It is thus of considerable importance, if we are to clarify the nature of interpretation, to understand the kinds of diverse activities the writing and study of literature may be. The *Iliad,* the *Odyssey,* the Pentateuch, the Gospels, the *Bhagavad Gita*—how astonishingly anonymous they all appear in this "scribbling age"!—these writings arose almost impersonally from a people in turn to shape that people and give it guiding ideals and understanding of life. Shelley thought that poets were unacknowledged legislators of the world. In the great epical and mythical works of world literature we discern poets, however anonymous they appear to be, as the acknowledged legislators of the world. Their works exercised a religious function, if we mean by that shaping the various activities of human life and persuading us of some defined vision of our significance as individuals. They contain the *exempla* and the truths necessary for the existence of a people, what it needs to know for orienting it in the world. But as de Rougement observed:

> In our day, Rilke forms only individual sensibilities in an elite of all classes. Flaubert tests the rhythm of his sentences in his *gueuloir* and what he corrects in them is only a matter of the ear, entirely subjective. But the reader of the sacred book of the *Mahabharata* risks going to sleep forever if he gets one syllable wrong![6]

Of course, we welcome the virtual disappearance of the superstitious awe for the sacred text which puts the inattentive reader under the immediate threat of divine retribution. Occasionally I have run into a student who must have mispronounced some sacred text or other and who clearly has been punished by perpetual somnolence. The magical attitude toward the text survives these days among some Orthodox Jews and Christian fundamentalists. The text is so sacred that even acknowledged errors are preserved, to be corrected by the reader at each reading; in the case of fundamentalists, the text cannot be interpreted at all. Some contemporary quarrels among literary critics are perhaps not as far from superstitious awe as we might imagine. Selected authors, ordinary mortals after all, have been virtually canonized, and selected texts have been subjected to analysis so minute that the classic master of Pilpul or the most ingenious of scholastics might well have to defer to these secular contemporary exegetes.

To be sure, modern literature still performs some of its immemorial functions. We do find in our great novelists and poets a moral criticism of life. Even when written in hostility to the surrounding culture, modern literature does offer models of what we may emulate or avoid. Our writers do articulate ranges of sentiment and experience formerly inchoate. But the literature of our time gives expression, as it must, to the moral and intellectual pluralism of modern culture. It cannot be otherwise at a time when many truths and many values contend with one another. Inescapably, the modern writer presents us with a personal view of the world, his authority derived simply from his own assumption of authority. In effect, each writer tells us that every man must work out his own salvation. It is surely no accident that anonymous literature has virtually disappeared from our world, for the individual's diffraction of common experience, however laden with insight, has replaced the wisdom of the collective. The normative has yielded to the idiosyncratic, the mythical imagination has given way to realism, whether that kind of realism purporting to describe the social process objectively, or the subjective psychological realism that would exhaust the content of a single consciousness. These apparently antithetical approaches to the "real" are really closely united, for the observer of social realities must sooner or later enter the minds of his characters if he is to interpret society.

The most important characteristic of modern literature which distinguishes it from anything in the past is that it is relentlessly critical of society and of culture itself, even the high culture which it may represent. As Lionel Trilling observed in a now classic essay, one of the most powerful and insistent themes of modern literature is the "disenchantment of our culture with culture itself."[7]

From this point of view, modern literary and humanistic culture is created by an elite that is hostile to the surrounding culture. The hellenistic literary elite, Greek or Roman, possessed a confidently aristocratic view of culture itself. They were free of the romantic illusion that there exists a true self which remains when culture is removed. The self, in fact, was like a work of art, and culture was the artist. Hence, they had no reason to question the value of culture and found every reason to be indifferent to the other cultures of the populations of the Empire. But the modern writer is under the constraints of the democratic ideology whether he will or no. That ideology is now everywhere, even in the most tyrannically governed societies; its fundamental axiom is that a cultural good must be measured by its capacity to be widely and easily distributed. Such notions have really very little to do with the essentials of government or with the preservation of political freedom. In fact, the socialist realism in art so long mandated as the official art of the communist governments is the most flagrant instance of this principle. To the extent that such an attitude is widely diffused in popular culture, the modern writer and artist must feel ill at ease as the member of a cultural elite. He cannot do what he must and serve the community as a whole.

Religious culture and the semisecularized humanistic culture which succeeded it assumed the task of shaping the imaginative and hence moral life of whole peoples. Such was its avowed aim. This task has now been assumed by mass culture with all the machinery we have come to know as the "media." To say this is to utter the most platitudinous of truths, but it has to be said if only because it is so obvious. The restriction of the literary and humanistic culture to an elite was accompanied, if not caused by, the appearance of new social realities created by the urbanization and industrialization of great peoples. New kinds of cleavages appeared in the culture. The newly emergent society, confident of its powers, could find no truly functional place for the poet, artist, or thinker. Art very rapidly became "fine art" and was relegated to museums, while the humanistically trained intellectual was gradually walled up in an ivory tower. I know that this view of how we got to where we seem to be is in need of massive qualifications. But there is little question that modern Western societies all demonstrate an enormous gulf between the values of the many and the values of the intellectual and artistic leaders.

If the intention of the authors of the Pentateuch was to remythologize the world for each successive generation, to shape and make continuous the common moral imagination of a people, the task of its interpreters was to preserve the vast matrix of meaning and value in the sacred text while rendering it intelligible and continually applicable to the changing circumstances and consciousness of the people. The modern author would seem to take a directly opposite tack and so, in a way, do many of his interpreters. The authors aim to strip away the fictions that overlay society and self to reveal hidden realities. The social and individual psychology of modern literature is thus a psychology of unmasking, and critics frequently pursue their authors with the same weapons the author has used on social and personal experience. The search for the true subject in the imagery of a poem or the deeper meaning of a novel parallels the author's search, real or assumed, for that truth which is hidden.

It is not simple realism, content with the facade of experience, which has dominated modern literature, but realism that seeks the real below the appearances of society and the appearances of self. In this sense, there is little difference between the objective realism of the social novel and the subjective realism of the so-called psychological novel. The locus of the real has shifted from society to self in the first intention only, for the analytic penetration of society leads by necessity to the analytic unmasking of the self.

The depoeticizing of the literary imagination in the interests of the real truth about the social or the psychic process seems like one of those revolutions achieved in the name of reason which bring in their train new kinds of unreason to replace the ones that were overthrown. How real is the social reality conveyed in even the greatest of realistic novels? Is the stream of consciousness ever a faithful transcription of psychic reality? Can art be altogether free of convention, of regulatory fictions, of the distinction between what is directly expressed and what is hinted at, free from unspoken assumption or euphemism? Of course not, and no writer of distinction ever thought so.

Conventions are much more like biological adaptations than logical propositions. They are assumptions we make or things we do in order to get on about important tasks. They are as unavoidable as euphemisms. There would appear to have been no time in history when the freedom to express some ignored aspect of reality was not accompanied by the introduction of fresh conventions, a sign not only of our need of shared fictions for communication to take place but also a sign that the revelation of the new is accompanied by the obscuration of the old.

Each age, thus, has subjects which it must veil in euphemisms. It once was possible to say that the world was under the dominion of sin and death, or that the poor are always with you, or that old age is a burden, and be clearly understood. But when it was possible to do that, it was not possible to talk about the sexual or other biological functions in any but a veiled manner, at least not in mixed company, or in any company at all if you wished to be considered a perfect gentleman or a lady. Today candor about the physiological facts is everywhere in evidence. But we have not achieved such intoxicating liberty without a price. Who dares talk of the poor as other than the underprivileged, the aged as other than senior citizens? Sin has become sickness or maladjustment, and the true face of death has been covered with a thick cosmetic veil. The art and literature of the world has always had things of the greatest interest and importance to say about our experience, but has never done so except through the mode of indirect discourse, by creating an aesthetic distance between itself and its appreciators. The truth of art takes a hypothetical form, and the primary act we bring to it is the assumption of an "as-if."

Has the modern striving to eliminate the fiction, to capture the richness of individual reality or the fine structure of social processes, led us away from being able to express the inexhaustibility of human significance that the greatest art miraculously conveys? Hamlet is far more fictional than Andrei Volknosky—we are told far less about him in terms familiar to psychological and social realism—but Hamlet possesses meanings which extend deep into the mystery of the human will and consciousness. This sort of comparison is, I know, much like comparing chalk and cheese and it might imply that one modality of literature or art is without qualification superior to another. Such is not my intention. I merely wish to point to the possibility that the character realized in mythical and poetic terms (whenever in the course of history the culture nourishes such uses of the imagination) may by virtue of that fact alone possess the universality that reaches across the most profound historical transformations to an audience yet unborn.

Ortega y Gasset described the progress of modern art and literature as a progress in dehumanization, the gradual elimination from art of the representation of personality and its vicissitudes. We need not agree that this process is as ubiquitous as Ortega thought, or that a Yeats, a Picasso, or a Joyce can be easily comprehended in it. There is, nevertheless, a large measure of truth in this thesis that we may observe both in the art which is caviar to the general and in popular art. The ideal of impersonality is essential, if only to prevent art from degenerating into formless, effusive self-expression. It should not be confused with depersonalization, the effort to detach literary and artistic activity from the realm of the important and intimate concerns of the race. True, the worthiness of a subject does not assure that the final outcome will be a work of artistic or intellectual merit. The relation between what is socially or morally desirable and works of art or thought is surely complex. We certainly do not wish to be forced into the position of concluding, with Tolstoy, that *Uncle Tom's Cabin* is greater than Shakespeare because it is so obviously and impeccably moral. But a pure aestheticism or intellectualism will surely be ignored by virtue of having nothing to say that mankind finds important.

All changes in literature and art tend to call forth exegetical techniques appropriate to them. To the extent that art has become depersonalized and, more important, viewed that way, the corresponding exegetical system has appeared in structuralism. Originating largely in the work of Ferdinand de Saussure, the linguist, and adapted to the work of making sense of the puzzling narratives of primitive myth by Lévi-Strauss, it has not failed to enter the fields of psychoanalysis, cultural history, and literary or artistic criticism.

Structuralism would appear to be precisely that system of interpretation which ignores the personality of the author as it might reveal itself in style and the created personalities of his characters. It denies to authorial intent any authority whatever, and in this agrees with existentialist interpretation where the latter has been influenced by the scepticism of Heidegger and Gadamer about the possibility of historical understanding. Structuralists read the text as essentially composed of covert meanings which reveal the universal structure of the human mind and which appear regardless of any conscious intent of the author. An impersonal "it" thus speaks through us.

Obviously, to read literature in this way is to apply to the literary productions of civilized men a system of interpretation applied to primitive myths by Lévi-Strauss, with considerable success. At least, he has been able to make some sense out of the most seemingly illogical and incoherent stories we can find. But the result when this system of interpretation is applied to a novel or a poem is the same sort of structural meaning in a coherent work of art that is found in the incoherent myth. The primitive myth, in fact, is from this point of view better, for it reveals the fundamental structure of the mind in a clearer form that the secondary elaborations that civilized authors impose upon it. This result should not surprise us. There is an analogous psychoanalytic approach to literature which finds the same unconscious meanings in the work of a mediocrity or the work of Shakespeare, and rightly so. We have no reason to assume that the greatest intellects and the meanest rest on an essentially different substrate of psychic processes.

The structuralist interpreter thus becomes a kind of archeologist of the spirit, digging through layer after layer of later civilization to discover a primary structure on which all successive structures have built and on which they rest. We may discern here a kind of theoretical validation of what we have sometimes seen in practice, before the theory was advanced. We have witnessed that new way of reading the Greeks, for example, for what remains of the primitive in their works. Some of us seem to find them more interesting for their unresolved relation to the irrational or the archaic than for the successes in domesticating the residues of the primitive past. Following Frazer, we may read Ovid less for his expression of urbane civilized values than for his keeping, unintentionally, a partial record of primitive beliefs.

It is very easy to misrepresent structuralist theory and exegetical practice if only because it is difficult to be certain you understand them. The writings of Lévi-Strauss and other luminaries of this movement are certainly written in an obscurity of style I can only call Delphic. Page after page seems portentous and fateful, laden with much that we want to understand if we could but unriddle it. The Sibylline oracles originally contained a complete prophetic record of the future, but the book came unbound, the leaves were scattered in the wind, and no one was ever able to put them back together in the right order. This ancient story has sometimes come to mind during my readings among the structuralists.

In any case, I cannot see how to avoid the conclusion that one is to read the *Divine Comedy* or *King Lear* in the same way as one might read Gilgamesh or the transcriptions made by anthropologists of the myths of the Brazilian Indians. All are in principle decipherable as a code of a binary character, the elements of which are removed from their place in any "surface" logic the text may possess and arranged according to binary oppositions which express the fundamental contrasts of human life, the oppositions between nature and culture, life and death.

From this point of view, all works have a common skeleton, and we read them at their primary level by peering through the frail flesh with the X-ray of structuralism. This may be, and probably is, the only way to make sense of primitive myth, just as psychoanalytic interpretation is the only way to make real sense of dreams. But only primitives and anthopologists really like their myths to remain primitive. Plato, Dante, and a lot of artists, poets, and philosophers preferred more informed uses of myth.

Structuralists, like some psychoanalysts and Marxists, seek to uncover a rock-bottom reality or structure which resides in man and is manifest in every human creation. The assumption is that once we discern this structure we have the universal text from which all other texts derive. The result is often literature and art so depersonalized that they become, like society itself, simply the raw material for a reductive analysis. The very aspect of literature and interpretation which generates new meanings, or transmits a morally complex vision of life, is bypassed and rendered irrelevant. It was a new critic and not a structuralist who thought that Milton's *Lycidas* was really about water, but that conclusion would not have been rejected by his successors.

We may observe that while this procedure has its validity for linguistics and anthropology, humanists should not simply assume that language exists simply to reveal its structure. It is surely legitimate to go along with Freud and interpret various puzzling phenomena as explicable in reference to unconscious contents of the mind which generate them. It is also legitimate to follow Lévi-Strauss or Lacan and seek the unconscious structure of the mind and not its unconscious contents. But the actual uses of language in art, science, and society are not innocent of moral intention, or instruction, or of intellectual implication. Every statement of fact, as Goethe observed, is already implicitly a statement of theory, and, we might add, every statement of value is also implicitly a judgment.

Erich Auerbach, after a lifetime of distinguished work in historical and humanistic scholarship, defined the common measure of the humanistic enterprise by saying that the study of the humanities is finally the study of personality. This was the fundamental assumption of the interpreters and creators of our humanistic legacy at least until recent times. I believe it will remain the assumption in the future.

Myth and Science in the Theology of Rudolf Bultmann

In 1896, ANDREW D. WHITE published his *A History of the Warfare of Science with Theology in Christendom*, a work of remarkable erudition based on years of what I can only call "penitential" reading, considering the kind of sources with which White had to deal. It was and perhaps still is the most important work of American scholarship intended to enlighten by means of scientific thought and to free its readers from any lingering attachments to supernaturalism, superstition, and dogmatism. White's main thesis is simple and is conveyed with the moral fervor worthy of a missionary: man's refusal to give up his theological ideas and beliefs resulted in continual interference with the progress of the enlightening truths of science and has been the cause of the "direst evil" in the moral, social, and political life of mankind. But this work is by no means a contribution to the rise of modern paganism, secularism, or "scientism." It is marked by a concern for the highest ethical values, for "true religion," a concern that might give it place alongside the works of Mill, Arnold, and Huxley.

Magical practices, the belief in demons, witches, and other supernatural agencies, fundamentalistic readings of the Bible are by no means extinct. The recent enormous success of a thoroughly vulgar film on demonic possession (1974), which even managed to secure the services of a few Jesuits as technical advisors, is surely one sign of that fact. On the other hand, Catholic, Protestant, and Jewish theologians are largely con-

cerned with providing interpretations of the Bible and of dogmatic and credal traditions which will be intelligible to cultivated
minds and in harmony with modern scientific and historical ways
of thought, or at least not in violent conflict with them.

The most influential of the modern exegetical methods employed to achieve these ends is that inaugurated by Rudolf
Bultmann, demythologizing—a term which perhaps sounds
more plausible as the original German "Entmythologiesie-
rung." Bultmann was a prodigious historical scholar as well as
a theologian whose studies and methods have become part of
the armamentarium of every modern biblical scholar. Even
those who cannot follow him to his conclusions must reckon
with the problems he poses and the exegetical crisis he defines.
I use the expression "exegetical crisis" because, in Bultmann's
view, the course of modern science and modern historical
thought have profoundly altered the theologian's task if—and
this is of the greatest importance—the theologian thoroughly
accepts the validity of scientific method and results as well as
the results of modern historical scholarship.

For Bultmann, science started to challenge the beliefs and
conceptions enshrined in the mythological view of the world
since its beginnings in ancient Greece. Modern science has
vastly extended the domains of experience brought under its
methods of inquiry and has progressively rendered the mythological view of the operations of nature or the psyche unbelievable. Taking from ancient science its conception of the world as
governed by cause and effect, more and more of what once
might have been left to "freedom," or chance, or supernatural
intervention has been subsumed by modern scientific thought
under the laws of natural necessity. Bultmann knows, too, that
modern conceptions of chance in physics do not, in fact, alter
the principle of causality in any essential way, and even if they
modify that principle, chance in modern physics certainly does
not allow for supernatural interruptions of the course of nature.

We shall return to Bultmann's concept of myth, but for the
moment we may accept tentatively his definition of myth as an
attempt to discuss other-world, transcendent realities in terms
of the events, persons, and realities of this world. As we shall
see, myth for Bultmann discloses truth of great moment, but

the growth of science and historical scholarship have served to make the literal myth a stumbling block rather than the vehicle of transcendence it once was.[1]

The term "myth" has come to be used in so many senses and so much controversy has surrounded it that it is difficult to use the term precisely without incurring the wrath of one or another mythographer. It appears, for example, in the writings of literary critics inspired by Kant or Coleridge as well as among those who draw upon Nietzsche, Freud, Jung, the Cambridge school of classical anthropologists, or, of course, Frazer. Its significance among the critics may vary from a psychological one to an anthropological one to a philosophical meaning that has little to do with either of the other perspectives. At the risk of repetition, I will briefly consider some current views of myth in order to locate Bultmann's position.

Myth sometimes seems to mean little more than a generally shared ideology: the Marxist myth, the Freudian myth, the myth of the state, and the like. Apparently, this manner of describing ideological systems allows an investigator to spare himself any rigorous consideration of whether or not the particular ideology in question is true, or to what degree it may be true. There is a certain legitimacy to this way of viewing systems of belief, for men do in fact live by fictions as well as truths. Indeed, illusions and fictions may well serve to order life, make men happier, and enable them to lead more effective lives.

Something of this view of the effectiveness of myth, despite its truth or lack of it in rigorously rational terms, may be found in Jung's work. Jungians, persuaded of the existence of a monomyth of vital psychobiological importance, seek in the religions, mythologies, and poetry of the world for greater or lesser approximations to the single universal story. The figures of myth and their vicissitudes are personifications of psychic process which elude other, more abstract, modes of description. Jungians propose, in fact, what appears to be an archetypal, psychological equivalent of a universal revelation. For them it is quite literally true that it is the same hero who possesses a thousand faces.

Others say that a story of general importance to a particular society is also a myth. Thus, Ahab's hunt for the white whale or Huckleberry Finn's journey down the river are myths. Apparently such stories are viewed as paradigmatic of some universal pattern of life's challenges and opportunities, and this makes them myths. Or they may be myths because they correspond to an archetypal pattern in a more subjective and psychological sense.

By no means is the term "myth" always applied to narrative. The highly metaphorical patterning of history and psychological dispositions we find in Yeats' *A Vision* or the later books of Blake are also myths.

A story explaining a ritual is certainly a myth for anthropologists, but no one any longer accepts the thesis that myths originate exclusively from ritual. It is abundantly clear that many myths are not associated with rituals at all. Lévi-Strauss' structural analysis of myth ignores the overt narrative content of myth and locates in the "deep" structure of myth its purpose of resolving contradictions in experience. This universal function of myth is apparent only in structural analysis wherein the elements of myth, detached from their narrative concatenations, are related to each other in a binary system of contradictions and oppositions and resolutions. This binary system is the underlying structure of any myth. The surface narrative must, so to speak, be broken up so that we may clearly perceive the opposing elements in the binary mythic fabric and how the course of narrative moves toward their mediation. Lévi-Strauss' method is explicitly parallel to the method of structural linguistics, but it has been observed that such a method applied to myth ignores the explicit mythic content. We might object if a linguist said that the true purpose of language was the revelation of its syntax; likewise, we could object to some of Lévi-Strauss' interpretations that what the myth says overtly is being ignored. However, in practice if not in principle, Lévi-Strauss does deal with mythic content.

Lévi-Strauss is rightly regarded as the thinker since Freud to have made the most original contribution to the study of myth, but his arcane and frequently exasperating stylistic obscurity has not helped persuade his readers that he has the key to the meaning of myth. Indeed, it is doubtful that all the various cultural phenomena denominated as myth can ever be accounted for by a single unified hypothesis, and Lévi-Strauss' theories work best on the cultures of his special concern. Paul Ricoeur has remarked that the structuralist interpretation of myth does not work very well for classical and Hebraic myths (the reply to this objection is that such myths have been subjected to secondary revisions and elaborations). Clearly, if this is the case, the theologian, the scholar of religion, literature, and art may not be able to make much more use of the theories of Lévi-Strauss than they of the similarly reductive theories of Freud or Jung.

To view all myth as reducible to a psychological process of resolving experiential dilemmas is *mutatis mutandis* quite similar to Freud's reduction of myth to a symbolic expression of the great primitive dramas of childhood, a product of the mind which emanates largely from the unconscious, a kind of waking dream work. In a sense, both Freud and Lévi-Strauss present myth as dealing with problems and expressing conflicts and their resolution, although the locus of the problem is quite different in each case. But Freud, while realizing that much of the great art of the world is rooted in myth, explicitly denied that psychoanalysis could resolve the problem of artistic value and meaning. Psychoanalysis could furnish the archeology of myth and symbol, but could not analyze the artist's power to transform the original material into something possessing a new significance.

Neither excessively wide interpretations of myth nor reductive interpretations can serve the purposes of the theological or philosophical exegete. Bultmann's view of myth has been criticized both by those interested in the elimination of myth from religion and those who would refuse to interpret religious myth at all. Yet Bultmann's definition of the mythical, as we shall see, is legitimate and should be allowed to stand. If myth is not always associated with religious concerns, a great deal of mythology is surely concerned with religious questions and expressive of religious views. I might paraphrase Bultmann and say that for him myth is expressed in a narrative which gives an account of what the cosmos is like and what man's place and destiny are in that cosmos. Myth, at least religious myth, conveys a pattern of events and an understanding of the order of things taken to be of vital and central significance. Although "religion" is a term as easy to conjure with as "myth," myth does lie within the sphere of religious concerns, does often convey a particular understanding of the problem of existence, and may elicit our commitment in one form or another. Although the language of myth is metaphorical, symbolic, and certainly anthropomorphic and animistic, it may resolve the dilemmas of life, the puzzling questions of its meaning.

>   Myth is an expression of man's conviction that the source and limit of the world in which he lives, i.e., the world which he knows and which is at his disposal, are to be sought not in it but beyond it, and that this area which he knows and has at his disposal is perpetually dominated and threatened by the uncanny powers which are its source and limit. Myth is therefore an expression of man's awareness that he is not lord of his own being. He is dependent not only within the known world, but more especially on those powers which hold sway beyond the confines of the known, and in this state of dependence he can be freed from the powers which he knows.[2]

The problem of such a view is best considered through a direct examination of the results of Bultmannian exegesis, but before we do so, we should briefly consider the views of Karl Jaspers, Bultmann's most acute philosophical critic, who is so persuaded of the autonomy of myth that he maintains the mythic is essentially impervious to any final exegesis at all.

According to Jaspers, to argue that Scripture must be demythologized because it is literally inconsonant with the scientific view of the world is to make two errors. The first is to accept the erroneous belief that mythical thought can ever be superseded at any time in history, past, present, or future. Mythical thinking for Jaspers is a permanent and valuable faculty of the mind, however ambiguous it may be. It is the primary way in which man experiences what Jaspers calls the "transcendent" and the "unconditioned." True, the "materialization" of myth has led to dogmatism, intolerance, horrendous threats against "unbelievers," all of the evils of religion which

White catalogued. But properly understood, mythical thought is indispensable to the proper working of the mind.

Bultmann's second error, according to Jaspers, rests on a mistaken view of science. Science cannot, as Bultmann holds, create a world view in any sense of that vague expression. The universal truths that science discovers are valid only from the point of view of abstract thought. Man cannot and never has lived concrete existence in terms of a scientific *Weltanschauung*. Such abstractions have no existential power simply because the statements of science are neither historical nor stated in historical terms. Men do not live, suffer, exult, and die by defining themselves in terms of a strictly scientific account of reality. Moreover, Bultmann mistakes the source of contemporary unbelief. Modern religious scepticism is not simply a result of scientific progress. Mythical and religious thought found its rationalistic critics long before there was any science to speak of.[3]

In the last analysis, myth should be taken for what it is, not rendered literally and not interpreted either, at least not in the light of philosophical and scientific knowledge. Myth carries meanings, for Jaspers, which can only be carried in mythical language. The symbols of myth are simply not translatable into any other kind of language. They can only be understood in their own mythical element, and they cannot be replaced by other meanings, for their meaning is unique. Only a new myth can interpret the old one, and that only by transforming old myth. Myth alone interprets myth.[4]

If one assumes the kind of exegetical nihilism that Jaspers argues, Bultmann's efforts are neither useful nor necessary, and extended to works of literature and art, they imply the dissolution of any attempt to render an account of our understanding of such works. But Bultmann makes a better case for his view of the relation between science and myth, and for demythologizing, than Jaspers is prepared to allow.

Bultmann's thought on the relation of myth to science takes its departure from the contrast between the view of the world and man expressed in the Bible and the view of the world and man derived from science. This contrast, although sharpened in modern times, goes back to antiquity, and Bultmann is emphatic that the two ways of thinking, mythological and scientific, come into opposition with the beginnings of critical and methodical inquiry into the nature of things in ancient Greece. In this respect, Bultmann anticipates the criticism of Jaspers. Science finds its beginnings when the pre-Socratics develop the notion of the *arche* or originating principle of the world, that principle which enables us to grasp a multiplicity of things as a unity. A further fundamental principle of both ancient and modern science is the concept of *cosmos,* the idea of order and harmony which arises from the search for grand uniformities and overarching principles governing the natural world of change. Both of these conceptions imply that the investigator of nature offers reasons (*logoi*) for the generalizations he makes about the world. Despite the vast differences between modern and ancient science, these principles have an abiding validity, and even the changes that have taken place and continue to take place in scientific understanding derive from the very stability of its way of looking at the world.[5]

Both upholders of the Ptolemaic and Copernican theories united in the notion of trying to understand the universe in terms of laws of nature accessible to reason. For the scientist of antiquity, and *a fortiori* for the modern man whose life has been so shaped by science and technology, reality essentially means what can be explained as rational in terms of a rational order of things. Although the great majority of modern men, even in advanced societies, have far from an adequate grasp of scientific thought, they are surrounded by the world that modern technology has generated and look in large measure to technology for their comforts, necessities, and to alleviate their suffering and pain.

Bultmann does not sufficiently distinguish between science and its technology, but there is no doubt that technology has raised the threshold of expectation of many millions of people and has rationalized much of life even in those not averse to irrational ways of dealing with the world. After all, even if a modern man prays for rain he will also try at the same time to seed clouds. Essentially, it is this transformation of consciousness which has made the mythological world view expressed in the New Testament unacceptable to Bultmann's modern man. He no longer finds a reflection of his own nature there, but instead finds it in the great works of modern literature, if he has been trained to read them, or in the mass cultural forms of literature and art.

Modern historical consciousness has also worked against our understanding of the mythological or biblical view of man and the world. Neither the modern historian nor the modern scientist will allow for intrusions of the supernatural into his scheme of things. As nature is a whole governed by laws of causality, so history is a self-contained whole. Its course differs from the course of nature because we discern in the flow of history forces or agents which affect the human will. Although we may not apply physical notions of causation to the historical process, we nevertheless look for this-world motives in the agents of historical change. To discern anything providential in the course of history is to see it with the eyes of faith; it is not to find empirical evidence for the divine working, for in any objective sense there is none.

Now religion and a great deal of our poetry and art state themselves in mythical and symbolic terms. The Romantic movement in literature is the most recent manifestation, on a universal scale, of a literary movement which views the imagination, the mythical, and symbolic as avenues to truth and as essential definitions of poetry. Bultmann's concern with the mythic in religion certainly presupposes this great European movement. His critique of religious myth is, to be sure, radical: he is undertaking a critique of mythical thought as such and not simply trying to prune the mythological excesses from the Sacred Text. He is the heir of Romantic thinkers and poets like Herder and Novalis in that, however different his conclusions, the mythic is viewed as a whole, as a unique, self-contained way of thought, and not simply as a psychic product subject to rationalization. Bultmann is close to his Romantic forebears, too, in wishing to conserve and not eliminate myth, and his exegetical method is intended to interpret myth in the interest of preserving not eliminating it.

Indeed, Bultmann is firm in refusing to accept any exegetical principles which eliminate myth. The heart of the Christian proclamation, the *kerygma,* is *in* the myth, not something we find by eliminating it. This proclamation is not a summons to mystical religious experience, nor is it a moral or philosophical truth of one kind or another. The New Testament speaks of an event through which God has brought about the redemption of mankind, although we need not assume a literalistic and factually historical view of precisely what that event was. Bultmann no more than Jaspers believes that dead bodies climb out of the grave. The true event lies in the possibility of existence disclosed in the faith that God intervened in the world to redeem mankind.[6]

The central importance Bultmann gives to eschatological mythology is indicated by his critique of the classic liberal theology of Harnack. In a preface to a reissue of Harnack's *What is Christianity?* Bultmann finds much to admire in Harnack's theological position, particularly the generosity and liberalism of his views and the monumental erudition that Harnack brought to the task of distinguishing what was of permanent significance in the Gospels from what was historically conditioned and part of the past. Bultmann, like other readers of Harnack, apparently admires the way he was both a prodigy of theological learning and a man who conserved a beautifully simple piety. For Harnack reminded us that the Gospel message is a message for all men and that it proclaimed the fatherhood of God and the brotherhood of man. He clearly recognized, too, that the believing interpreter must be "liberal," for we cannot always distinguish clearly between what is permanent and what impermanent in the Sacred Text, nor can pure erudition, however immense, decide on whether there has been a revelation and what its content is. Indeed, in a famous figure of speech, Harnack warned that the scriptural interpreter must not be like the child who, wanting to get at the kernel of a bulb, went on picking leaves until there was nothing left and then realized that it was just the leaves which made the bulb. I might add that such destructive interpretation is not uncommon with secular texts too.[7]

But Bultmann parts company with the great master even though they both agree that "religion is the power to escape from the power and service of the transitory." Bultmann notes that Harnack's error lay in simply interpreting away as a residue of the past all of the "strangeness" of the New Testament, precisely the eschatological and gnostic mythical motifs which must, to be sure, be "demythologized," but which are the vehicles for the existential appropriation of faith. In effect, Harnack was too much of a "humanist." He found too easy an accommodation between his large Goethean view of life and culture and the Gospels.

There is, I think, a measure of truth in this critique of Harnack, yet towards the end of his book we find a memorable passage on the relation between knowledge and faith which Goethe could never have written.

> Gentlemen, it is religion, the love of God and neighbour, which gives life a meaning; knowledge cannot do it. Let me, if you please, speak of my own experience, as one who for thirty years has taken an earnest interest in these things. Pure knowledge is a glorious thing, and woe to the man who holds it light, or blunts his sense for it. But to the question, whence, whither, and to what purpose, it gives an answer today as little as it did two or three thousand years ago. It does, indeed, instruct us in facts; it detects inconsistencies; it links phenomena; it corrects the deceptions of sense and idea. But where and how the curve of the world and the curve of our own life begins—that curve of which it shows us only a section—and whither this curve leads, knowledge does not tell us.[8]

Thus we might say that Harnack ignores the strangeness of the New Testament while Bultmann finds it essential and interprets it. This difference in exegetical practice rests on a number of further differences between them. Is religion essentially an escape from the world, or a way of integrating oneself with life and the world? These two alternatives need not exclude each other, depending on the emphasis and interpretation one gives to one or another pole of this antithesis. To the extent that Bultmann seems to emphasize a kind of detachment or escape from the world as the aim of religion, he may well have been prompted by the conditions in Germany. But Harnack, working in happier times, also acknowledges the function of religion to be transcendence over all that comes into being and passes away, even though he might not advocate escaping from the world in any radical sense.

Can the mythical element in Scripture—so much of it foreign to our way of thinking, some of it both intellectually and morally repugnant—be made to yield the kind of sophisticated meanings Bultmann discovers in it? Can we ignore in our interpretations the overt intentions of the original myth makers and myth bearers and find a suitable existential significance divorced, in the last analysis, from what the authors of Scripture and countless believers have assumed as in large measure literally true? If so, in what way does the truth of revelation lie behind what it literally says? Both Bultmann and Harnack agree on the necessity of interpretation and on the fact that the truth is not in the letter but in the spirit, in some meaning of that great phrase—but how? Which of the documents of revelation may be safely discarded as belonging to the debris of history and what is essential to conserve? Lastly, is Christianity essentially a moral or an existential possibility in religion?

Harnack, of course, wanted to eliminate myth from the New Testament quite as much as he wanted to eliminate dogma from the act of faith. It has been justly observed that his superb *History of Dogma* is the greatest work of scholarship ever undertaken by a historian essentially hostile to his subject. Harnack, in fact, sought a sublime simplification of the Gospels and of the massive attempt of Christian thought to state itself in the categories of Greek philosophy. The history of dogma, for Harnack, was the result of the hellenization of Christianity and, like the mythical elements of Scripture, obscured the essence of Christianity.[9]

In some respects, as we have seen, there is nothing novel in a theological concern with the problem of myth. Allegorical interpretation, however "mythological" a lot of the interpretations of the Alexandrian fathers might seem to us, was an attempt to eliminate received myths as objective statements where they were found to be either morally or intellectually unpalatable. In modern times, the concept of myth was introduced into biblical scholarship at the end of the eighteenth century where it was thought to be a device deliberately employed by Jesus and his disciples to accommodate their exalted teachings to the limited capacities of their contemporaries. To eliminate the mythological from the New Testament was thus to fulfill the intentions of the founders of Christianity. This view of myth derives directly from the old theory of accommodative metaphor in Scripture and is characteristic, in part, of those "enlightened" theologians who, in the tradition of men like Locke, were concerned to show the "reasonableness of Christianity." The inauguration of modern historicism and the revaluation of the mythological which took place during the Romantic period soon persuaded biblical scholars that, whatever the status of myth, the biblical writers believed the myths they were expressing. This realization did not change the conviction among liberal theologians that myth had to be eliminated. Strauss undertook this elimination of myth in the interest of disclosing the Hegelian absolute idea. Modern liberal theology also eliminated myth as an historically conditioned mode of expression and found, with Harnack, a simple revelation of the fatherhood of God, the brotherhood of man, and the infinite worth of the human soul.

The "history of religions" school of theologians deepened our understanding of just how profoundly mythological, how "strange" if you prefer, the Bible really is. They, too, sought to eliminate myth and found the essentials of Christianity in the mystical life of the Christian community and in the mystical union with Christ as symbol of God.[10]

Bultmann differs from all of his predecessors on his insistence on conserving myth, and I should add, on the exegetical method derived from Heidegger, which permits him to disregard the authority of authorial intention. What this means is best discerned through a few examples. Myth in Bultmann's view arises from man's attempt to describe the other-worldly in terms of this world (*Der Mythos objectiviert das Jenseitige in Diesseitigen*). The myth maker may thus use spatial imagery for the notions of both the transcendence of God and the transcendence of evil. Enlighteners like White, or Lecky in his *History of European Morals,* or G. G. Coulton in *Five Centuries of Religion* regarded with indignation and contempt all notions of hell and demons. For Bultmann, hell and its citizens have lost all literal significance—regardless of what the original creators and believers may have thought—and hell stands revealed as a "space myth." In refusing the myth any literal significance, Bultman

stands firmly with the moral and intellectual ideas of enlightenment. In conserving the myth through an interpretation which
prescinds from authorial intention, he stands with an important
strain of Romantic thought: myth may emanate from individuals
but their significance transcends their source in the wishes,
hopes or fears of the individual psyche as such.

> When mythological thinking forms the conception of hell,
> it expresses the idea of the transcendence of evil as the
> tremendous power which again and again afflicts mankind.
> The location of hell and of men whom hell has seized is
> below the earth in darkness, because darkness is tremen-
> dous and terrible to men.[11]

Certainly there are other possible explanations for the idea
of hell. Science, in the person of a psychoanalyst, might well
see it as a projection of unconscious sadistic fantasies of infantile origin upon a cosmological screen, the product of the fears
and hatreds and wishes of childhood whose true origin remains
unconscious to the believer but which achieve expression in the
objective terms of the myth. From this psychoanalytical point
of view, this myth expresses the inner world in terms of this-
world imagery, while Bultmann conceives of the myth as expressing the other-world in terms of this world.

Bultmann chooses an existential interpretation and considers this particular "space myth" as referring to a structure
of existence. There is thus no occasion to suffer the moral
repugnance of a Lecky, the intellectual outrage of a White or
Coulton, which arises in dealing seriously with the literal
significance of the myth. Bultmann is thus able to pay his debt
to science, history, reason, and his moral sensibilities, at the
same time conserving the myth of hell in some significant way.
Science does not, for him, "unweave the rainbow." All it does
is create the need for the theologian to find the appropriate
method for his exegesis of the Sacred Text. No one can read
the scholarly writings of Bultmann without realizing his profound respect for the canons of reason, science, and scholarship. That the hell myth has been profoundly criticized, repudi-
ated, or accepted by untold numbers of the faithful, that it has
been the vehicle and rationale for numberless cruelties is

rendered irrelevant by detaching the myth from its historical context and function as well as the intention of its authors.

Along with "space myths," Christianity expresses its view of existence in a "time myth," the eschatological doctrine of Scripture. The last things referred to in eschatological doctrine are last in the course of time, when the judgment of God will be manifest and history as we know it will have an end. The eschatological myth sets this world of transience in time against eternity and expresses thereby the transcendence of God. Unlike the Greek conception of the limiting power of fate or *moira,* eschatological thought sees a temporal limit, the end-time, as coming in a great cosmic catastrophe which is no other than God's judgment upon sinful man. Although Jesus' eschatological preaching lacks the imagery of a happy time which supervenes upon the final catastrophe, such a blissful renewal of the world under the governance of God was a regular feature of Jewish apocalyptic. The apocalyptic myth portrays God as a personal judge, the omnipotent creator of the world who will, after judging it, renew it and bring it to the state it was to have in the original divine intention. Eschatology, like the Greek conceptions of *moira, hybris,* and *nemesis,* is a myth expressive of human limitation, but in addition to the moderation and resignation preached by Greek sages, it implies a summons to repentance, for man and the world are under the dominion of sin. In the eschatological myth, man is limited by his sinfulness and contrasted with the holiness of God, who is his creator and judge and who utterly transcends his condition.

> In the Israelite view of history the goal of history is promised, but the realization of the promise is conditional on the obedience of the people. In the apocalyptic view the end of history comes with necessity at the time determined by God. According to the first view, the course of history becomes clear by the knowledge of divine justice which guides history to its goal. In the second view, the course of history is revealed by the knowledge of the secret counsel of God. In the first view the responsibility of the individual coincides with the responsibility of the whole people, a responsibility in face of the future possibility of welfare *or* judgment. In the second view the individual is

responsible for himself only, because the end will bring welfare *and* judgment at the same time, and the individual's future will be decided according to his works.[12]

Thus, it is precisely where Harnack scoffed that Bultmann remained to pray. The mythology of the New Testament is precisely what contains the *kerygma,* the proclamation, the message which is meant to detach us from the world. If religion is meant to further self-development, and to improve the world, we can certainly find encouragement in major elements of Christian tradition. But the heart of the message is the detachment of "eschatological existence," not, be it noted, mystical detachment. Eschatological detachment is, unlike mysticism, a paradoxical state of existence. One does not escape from society, or the world, in any literal sense of the term; one is free from the world while remaining in it.

The New Testament message is thus essentially conveyed in two overarching myths and both of them are other-worldly: a Jewish eschatological myth and a Gnostic redemption myth. They share a common dualistic view of the world which sees the present age under the dominion of demonic forces, a world waiting to be redeemed. The world must wait because it cannot accomplish its own redemption. This is possible only by divine intervention, and both myths postulate such an intervention. The eschatological myth, as we have seen, is historical: the end-time has been inaugurated and the future will complete the eschatological drama. A cosmic catastrophe is imminent which will bring an end to the present age. The new age will begin or has begun with the appearance of the Messiah.

The Gnostic myth is not framed in a mythology of history, however. The dualism here is essentially not one of ages or aeons, but a dualism of a world of darkness and a world of light. A son of God sent from the world of light enters this world of darkness in the form of man and through his teachings and his life redeems the elect by opening the way back to their true celestial home. This is the myth of St. John's Gospel. Bultmann interprets the Gnostic myth as one which realizes, in spatial terms, the temporal eschatology of Jewish apocalyptic. The author of John, according to Bultmann, has in fact demythologized the eschatological expectation. Salvation is now.[13]

For Bultmann, the meaning of these myths lies not in the imagery in which they are expressed, but in their implicit understanding of human existence. This kind of interpretation is not to be confused with allegorical or typological interpretation. The latter deals with images, events, and persons and gives them meanings of a second order. Mythical events might be thus rendered as symbols of inner spiritual events, events of the soul. Or mythical imagery might be translated into a philosophical tenet. Bultmann's interpretation does not issue in a second-order system of symbols taken as the true meaning of the first-order system, a more intelligible rendering of the text. Interpretation issues in existential self-understanding and in existential decision or engagement. This self-understanding is not reducible to the terms of a scientific anthropology or ideology.

It is not, as I understand it, the kind of self-understanding which might be generated by a psychoanalyst interpreting a dream or a fantasy. It does not disclose to the interpreter something about his own human nature or that of others. It conveys a perception of being in the world which is appropriated in a decision to accept or to refuse. The myths are the unique vehicles for generating a particular attitude toward existence, one which demands decision because it challenges us to accept the light it sheds on the riddle of existence itself. In principle, other works of comparable religious authority or works of thought or imagination could indeed generate as profound a response. In practice, if the exegete responds to the New Testament, he has received "revelation" and so his response is both unique and exclusive.[14]

The demand for exegesis is not exhausted, however, by what modern thought has rendered unbelievable. A further challenge to the appropriation of the New Testament is posed by the way modern man understands himself. He experiences himself as a kind of unit, with ego boundaries. When he experiences acute inner division he interprets it as psychic disorder. Although man may know he is dependent, he does not assume that he is prey to supernatural powers external to himself. Psychology and biology teach the naturalist to understand the character of his dependence and so encourage a rational form of mastery and independence. The idealist may think that his true self is his consciousness, yet he accepts the fact that he is physically conditioned and thereby achieves another mode of rational mastery. To such men the workings of a supernatural spirit or the powerful workings of the sacraments are unintelligible. The effects of baptism or the Eucharist are either magical and therefore a sham, or to be explained by simple psychological principles. Moreover, the conception of death as punishment, a biblical doctrine of the greatest importance, strikes both the naturalist and the idealist as unintelligible. To the idealist death may be a problem, but it is not a punishment, while to the biologist death is no problem at all.

To say that biologists do not view death as a problem is perhaps an understatement. Prompted by the complex problems surrounding death and dying generated by a new medical technology, a considerable literature on death has come into being during the last ten or fifteen years. One result has been to explore the biological and cultural function of human death and to view it less as the great enemy than as the necessary presupposition of all biological and cultural evolution. Both the enormous drive to self-preservation and the inevitability of death are required for the preservation of life through evolution. If we are to save life, we must desire to live and so resist death, but we must also die as others did before us. This may, if you please, be seen as the fundamental tragic paradox of individual existence, but it involves a totally different view of death than that enshrined in Christian myth.

It is not only the notion of death as punishment, but the idea of physical resurrection of the dead and of vicarious atonement which violate our sense of what our lives as physical beings or moral agents are like. To appropriate immortality through someone else and to be declared innocent through the sufferings of someone else may be convenient ways of realizing these wishes, but they are simply not the way we think such possibilities can be realized. The ancient myths are strange, indeed, although perhaps not as obsolete from a psychological point of view as Bultmann thinks. The ultimate puzzle the theologian must solve is why, if salvation is the understanding of one's true self, it should have taken such a strange and now alien form.[15]

Bultmann's exegetical techniques apply to other than biblical myths. The Greek, i.e., Platonic, and the Christian views of death and immortality are both conveyed in mythical terms. Christian and Platonic eschatology concur in positing bliss after death, a supreme felicity which is to be understood as freedom. Plato's various and differing conceptions of the afterlife all express the notion of freedom as freedom of the soul, the true and indestructible self, freedom from the body and all that the body must itself suffer and inflict upon the soul imprisoned in it. After death, the soul enters a transcendent world beyond space and time, a world which is apprehended in philosophic dialogue and which may even be the realm of eternal dialogue, as Socrates suggests in the *Apology* (4lc). Hence, we are enjoined in Plato's *Phaedo* to practice dying.

The Christian view of post-mortem bliss is also freedom, but that freedom which man obtains when he recovers his true self, a self free from the dominion of sin and death. If Paul promises the believer perfection of knowledge (1 Cor. 13) in his magnificent hymn to love, the knowledge to be had is not knowledge as Plato would have understood it. Rather, the believer will achieve a clear, certain, direct relation to God. Purity of heart is the requisite for the vision of God and this vision is understood in some proportion to physical vision, for the soul in the Christian scheme of things is not the true man thrown into a physical body (Plato's *Phaedrus*), but the physical body will be replaced by a spiritual and incorruptible body at the resurrection. Blessedness is essentially untroubled worship of God in immediacy, the fulfillment of the wish of the pious, not the wish of the philosopher.

Bultmann, as these examples may serve to show, does not quite raise the problem of the relation between what the original myth makers and bearers may have made of the myth and what modern man must make of it. Certainly, we can assume that for the original believers what the myth says and what it may symbolize, in Frege's distinction between *Sinn* and *Bedeutung,* are not discriminated. Even if they cannot be said to have understood the myth "literally" in some crude sense of the term, the complex of meanings and references in the myth were certainly not discriminated. Mythical thought does not appear to make the distinction between what is literal and what is symbolic in that it is prior to such a distinction. When this distinction does arise, the myth bearer becomes a myth interpreter, and has recourse to analogical thought. A particular element in the myth may then suggest an analogy to be made between this world and another. With analogy we enter the realm of symbolism, and the user of symbols differs from the bearer of myth in his consciousness of the oblique character of his expression. Paul Tillich referred to this process as the "breaking of myth" and argued that, although myth should be clearly recognized as myth, religious myths should also be retained in their mythical form and not replaced with conceptual substitutes.[16]

The classical rationalism of White which envisioned science as a knight in armor doing battle against all the enslaving superstitions perpetuated in myths gives way in Bultmann to an image of science as a necessary achievement of the human spirit which constrains us to evolve a clearer conception of the inner meaning of religion and faith. Nevertheless, however necessary the scientific demythologizing of the world may be, and however useful a challenge it has presented to the theologian, science perpetuates the ancient Greek conception of the rational *Weltanschauung,* the ideal of a general system of nature in which man may find a proper place and self-definition. However unflattering such conceptions may be, and however small a value they might place on the individual's life in the great scheme of things, a man may well find the adoption of a complete "cosmology" of this sort tempting. According to Bultmann, we seek to evade the truth that man is man only as existence, as an historical, decision making, experiencing being. Science, as world-encompassing explanation, may offer us a false refuge from the anxiety attendant on existing in this sense. But faith can have no quarrel with any finding of science, only a quarrel with its claims to understand the purpose of being and to exhaust the meaning of man as man.

Science is thus for Bultmann a valid demythologizer in its own sphere, and it has done its work. What then is left of "faith"? Again, some examples of Bultmann's view of the relation between faith and science will give us the clearest understanding of his concept of faith and a more precise idea of just what Bultmann takes science to be.

For Bultmann, faith arises with the realization that the scientific world view does not encompass the totality of reality, either of the world or of human life. On the other hand, faith emphatically does not offer us an alternative world view. Demythologizing means precisely the elimination of world views, archaic or not, from faith. Faith recognizes that the world view of science is necessary for working in the world and even in the conduct of daily life. It is effectively true. To acknowledge the scientific world view is to acknowledge the solid reality of cause and effect and to conduct our lives in accordance with an understanding of that principle. But the closed universe of cause and effect leaves no room for an effective God. "This is the paradox of faith, that faith nevertheless understands as God's action here and now an event which is completely intelligible in its natural or historical connection of events. This nevertheless is inseparable from faith."[17]

This kind of denial is not to be confused with mythological denial or supernaturalistic denial of the universal order of cause and effect. Myth assumes a certain degree of natural order but one subject to continual and decisive interference by supernatural agencies. In Bultmann's meaning of faith, the affirmation of God denies the universal order as a whole. The whole of the scientific world view is denied in the eyes of faith. I take this to mean that, although there are no miracles as supernatural intrusions into the course of events, events may be viewed as miraculous. Although there are no evidences for the providential ordering of history, to the eyes of faith all of history may be viewed as salvation history. Such, I think, are the implications of Bultmann's view of faith. But if the God of faith is not visible in the scientific view of the world, neither is the self or one's personal existence. Affirmation of God, like affirmation of the unique, experiencing, irreducible self, denies the universal nexus of cause and effect as science understands it. If man is understood in the existential sense as a historical being, continually in concrete situations and continually deciding, then faith is not simply a psychological "objective" event, according to Bultmann. It is the perception of a realm of being outside

causality. This is true even if faith affirms the activity of God
where all scientific and philosophical thought would conspire to
show that this affirmation is an illusion. Self as well as the
"living God" are affirmed in a realm of being outside of the
"objectivity" of scientific thought. There can be no objective
proof for what faith affirms of God.[18]

> We can believe in God only in spite of experience, just as
> we can accept justification only in spite of conscience.
> Indeed, de-mythologizing is a task parallel to that per-
> formed by Paul and Luther in their doctrine of justification
> by faith alone without the works of the law. More pre-
> cisely, de-mythologizing is the radical application of the
> doctrine of justification by faith to the sphere of knowl-
> edge and thought. Like the doctrine of justification, de-
> mythologizing destroys every longing for security. There
> is no difference between security based on good works
> and security built on objectifying knowledge. The man
> who desires to believe in God must know that he has
> nothing at his disposal on which to build this faith, that he
> is, so to speak, in a vacuum.[19]

Man for Bultmann, in a manner reminiscent of Sir Thomas
Browne's definition of him as the "Great Amphibium" living in
divided and distinguished worlds, must live a paradox: "let
those who have the modern world-view live as though they had
none."[20]

We may well ask why man must live out this rather strenuous paradox. Not everyone would agree with Bultmann's view
of existence or human life, obviously, but even those sympathetic to his religious pieties might object to the abyss Bultmann
places between knowledge and faith. After all, natural theology,
cosmic piety of one form or another, still has its able defenders.
But on this point let us let Bultmann speak for himself:

> It is the word of God which calls man away from his
> selfishness and from the illusory security which he has
> built up for himself. It calls him to God, who is beyond the
> world and beyond scientific thinking. At the same time, it
> calls man to his true self. For the self of man, his inner
> life, his personal existence is also beyond the visible world
> and beyond rational thinking. The Word of God addresses

man in his personal existence and thereby it gives him freedom from the world and from the sorrow and anxiety which overwhelm him when he forgets the beyond. By means of science men try to take possession of the world, but in fact the world gets possession of men. We can see in our times to what degree men are dependent on technology, and to what degree technology brings with it terrible consequences. To believe in the Word of God means to abandon all merely human security and thus to overcome the despair which arises from the attempt to find security, an attempt which is always vain.[21]

In this passage we perceive one feature of Bultmann's view of science which is subject to considerable questioning. There is no doubt that modern science has sought not only the understanding of nature but also dominion of nature. The aspect of modern science which proclaims dominion is, of course, technology, but some of the moral chastening that we may get from religion may also come from science, if not from technology. Freud's *The Future of an Illusion* or *Civilization Its Discontents* offer a profoundly disenchanted view of the world and man's lot in it. Darwin's vision of the evolution of life and of man can be most depressing to sensitive spirits who are more comfortable with a view of the world somewhat closer to the heart's desire. Blake, among other poets of the Romantic period, was horrified by the Newtonian world machine and its clock maker God. In fact, science—and I do not mean technology—does not offer in its way of understanding the world any occasion for *hybris* or Promethean exaltation. It has, in its understanding of the world, perhaps been more frequently the cause of despair than encouragement to those clinging, even agnostically, to the older views of the world. Technology, of course, presents another face of science, and Bultmann correctly grasps the present rival to religious piety in spite of some disenchantment with it here and there. Technology does seek to conquer the world, even as historical religion has sought to conquer the world and by no means always in some transcendental sense. The ideology of both technology and religion is in essence unlimited in its dominion, but much science and religion too proclaim a doctrine of limits if we will but stay to understand. The ecological crisis or the energy crisis are nothing but the collision of technology with natural limitation and were predictable decades before they happened on the basis of scientific knowledge.

Indeed, it might well be argued that modern science implies a doctrine of limitation as forceful as the old limits placed upon man by the old gods delivering a nemesis to man's presumption and pride. Even the devious and subtle ways in which the gods took their revenge on men's attempts to escape their destined lot have been reproduced in the way in which we stumble from one unanticipated technological crisis to another. The Promethean image of science as knowledge died long ago, but the Promethean image of technology, which did powerfully exist, has also begun to fade. Technology has been and is an inevitable part of human existence and, in vastly heightened form, we are left with the old problem of controlling it. The benefits of technology and the hope it carries for the dispossessed majority of the world's population should not be ignored. Only the highly developed nations of the world have any experience of the negative effects of technology, and it should be observed that they still have abundant evidence of its benefits.

Bultmann's views of science and technology should not, however, be confused with current forms of irrationalism or antiscientism. As a theologian, he simply stands at the opposite pole from the great scholastics who sought to mediate rationally between science and faith and to reconcile them. He is sometimes strongly reminiscent of a latter-day version of an extreme medieval Averroist, when he virtually says that what is true in the scientific vision of the world may be completely denied by faith without denying the validity of the findings of science. Certainly there can be no rationally ascertainable relation between the scientifically ascertained working of the world and the relation of that world to the God Bultmann apprehends by faith. Not only is there no "natural theology" for Bultmann—the world is too much under the dominion of sin for us to find divine evidences in the creation as object of knowledge—but the viewpoint of faith inverts the scientific vision of things. It is perhaps this last point which inclines a reader to think of the medieval Averroists. Whether Heidegger's existentialism has rescued him from that paradoxical view of things is, to me, an open question. He has surely replaced the medieval paradoxes with some new ones.

Bultmann's work, however we may regard its results, remains the most ambitious and instructive interpretive effort of our time. Nietzsche—surely not a sympathetic critic of religion—called the Bible "the greatest of books." Coming from the most imaginative interpreter of classical culture in his time, this is indeed an accolade. Even desacralized and unchurched, the Bible remained a classic—*the* classic—in the sense that it addressed itself to our most important concerns although its origins are remote from us in time and place. To the interpreter of its universality, this book imposes the ultimate interpretive demands: he must combine the greatest possible learning with the greatest possible simplicity, the most ambitious acts of the historical imagination with the immediate apprehension of the most urgent concerns of his contemporaries. This is a requirement which the Bible may make which no other book makes in the same degree or in quite the same way. And this situation is not, as Nietzsche recognized, simply the outcome of historical accident or the religious history of a particular civilization. It derives from the "classic" quality of the text itself. These interpretive requirements are paradoxical and Bultmann, in accepting them, imposed a more strenuous paradox upon himself than any we can find in his conclusions.

Notes

Interpretation and Its Occasions

1. It has sometimes been argued that mathematics is not a suitable language for biology, and if one assumes that mathematics deals exclusively with the quantifying of experience, there is a large measure of truth to this stricture. Even as skilled a mathematical interpreter of nature as D'Arcy Thompson (*On Growth and Form,* 2nd ed., 2 vols., [Cambridge, 1942]) acknowledged as much. But combinatorial mathematics and topology, among other developing branches of mathematics, show great promise of having biological applications hitherto thought beyond mathematical power. There is a complex mathematical order underlying taxonomic relations and developmental change, but we have not as yet been able to find, in any great degree, a suitable mathematical language for it. That contributions of great significance to biology have been made and will continue to be made with little or no use of mathematics need not blind us to the desirability and possibility of a mathematical description of biological phenomena which now elude it.

2. There is an ever growing literature on scientific explanation and interpretation. Two volumes accessible to the non-scientist are Mary B. Hesse, *Models and Analogies in Science* (Notre Dame, Ind., 1966) and Thomas S. Kuhn, *The Structure of Scientific Revolutions,* 2nd ed. enlarged (Chicago, 1970). For the biological sciences, more technical than the above, see *Models and Analogies in Biology, Symposia of the Society of Experimental Biologists* 14 (Cambridge, 1960).

3. I ignore, of course, "deliberately" difficult works, such as *Finnegan's Wake,* for example. Although many literary works of the past might be worth a lifetime of dedicated study, I can't think of any writer, not Dante nor Milton, who demanded such a commitment from his reader as a *sine qua non* of entry into it.

4. R. G. Collingwood, *Outlines of a Philosophy of Art* (London, 1925), pp. 98–99.

5. (Paris, 1962), E. T.: *The Savage Mind* (Chicago, 1966).

6. For a debate among anthropologists concerning metaphor, symbol and the exegesis of ritual see the correspondence, with references, between James W. Fernandez and Victor Turner in *Science* 182, no. 28, (December 1973): 1366–67. Fernandez writes: ". . . the ritual system is, in essence, a system

155

of enacted correspondence. A metaphor (and related tropes) is the statement, explicit or implicit, of a correspondence between some subject of thought in need of clarification and an object which brings some clarity to it. Metaphor, not symbol, should be considered the basic analytic unit of ritual because ritual and ritual symbols spring from metaphors. . . . A metaphor is an image predicated upon a subject by virtue of some sense of apt correspondence perceived in the culture, and it is this image which is efficacious on the subject's experience and in planning his performance in the ritual process."

7. A good account of Heidegger's exegetical methods can be found in the essays included in *The New Hermeneutic,* ed. James T. Robinson and John B. Cobb (New York, 1964), and in Paul J. Achtemeier, *An Introduction to the New Hermeneutic,* (Philadelphia, 1969). Lévi-Strauss is a copious and difficult writer. The best introduction to structuralism I know can be found in the essays included in Michael Lane's *An Introduction to Structuralism* (New York, 1970). Lane's book includes some work of Lévi-Strauss. The most accessible of Lévi-Strauss' writings is *Structural Anthropology,* trans. C. Jacobson and B. Grundfest Schoepf (New York, 1963). An excellent analytical account of his work may be found in G. S. Kirk, *Myth: Its Meaning and Functions in Ancient and Other Cultures,* (Cambridge, 1970). On psychoanalytic interpretation one should consult the admirable reference work of J. Laplanche and J. B. Pontalis, *The Language of Psychoanalysis,* trans. Donald Nicholson-Smith, under the entries "symbolism," "symbol," "primary process and secondary process," etc.

8. There is an admirable short history of biblical exegesis by R. M. Grant, *A Short History of the Interpretation of the Bible,* rev. ed. (London, 1965). See also the various articles in the *Cambridge History of the Bible,* 3 vols. (Cambridge, 1963–70), and the penetrating remarks of Rudolf Bultmann, *Theology of the New Testament,* 2 vols. (London, 1952 and 1955). 1:108 ff.

9. See the penetrating study of Arthur Darby Nock, *Conversion: The Old and New in Religion from Alexander the Great to Augustine of Hippo* (Oxford, 1933), especially pp. 164 ff.

10. A number of other such examples are given in Beryl Smalley, *The Study of the Bible in the Middle Ages,* 2nd ed. (Oxford, 1952; Notre Dame, Ind., 1964).

11. See the remarkable study of Gnosticism by Hans Jonas, *The Gnostic Religion: The Message of the Alien God and the Beginnings of Christianity,* 2nd ed. (Boston, 1963), especially pp. 91 ff: "Instead of taking over the value-system of the traditional myth, [Gnosticism] proves the "deeper" knowledge by reversing the roles of good and evil, sublime and base, blest and accursed, found in the original. It tries not to demonstrate agreement, but to shock by blatantly subverting the meaning of most firmly established, and preferably also the most revered, elements of tradition. The rebellious tone of this type of allegory cannot be missed, and it therefore is one of the expressions of the revolutionary role which Gnosticism occupies in late classical culture." See also R. M. Grant, *Gnosticism and Early Christianity* (New York, 1959); J. Knox, *Marcion and the New Testament* (Chicago, 1942); A. Von Harnack, *Marcion: Das Evangelium vom Fremden Gott,* 2nd ed. (Leipzig, 1924).

12. Cf. the remarks of Northrop Frye, *The Anatomy of Criticism* (Princeton, 1957), pp. 126, ff. Schleiermacher's hermeneutical writings are conve-

niently available in Heinz Kimmerle's edition, Fr. D. E. Schleiermacher, *Hermeneutik* (Heidelberg, 1959).

13. See E. H. Lenneberg, *Biological Foundations of Language*, with appendices by Noam Chomsky and Otto Marx (New York, 1967).

14. For a general study of the modern hermeneutical tradition see Richard E. Palmer, *Hermeneutics: Interpretive Theory in Schleiermacher, Dilthey, Heidegger, and Gadamer* (Evanston, Ill., 1969).

15. See the brilliant study of E. D. Hirsch, *Validity in Interpretation* (New Haven, 1967), especially chap. 4.

16. See Martin Heidegger, *Being and Time*, trans. John Macquarrie and Edward Robinson (New York, 1962), par. 31, pp. 54 ff.; Rudolf Bultmann, "New Testament and Mythology," in *Kerygma and Myth* 1, 2nd ed. (London, 1964), and "The Problem of Hermeneutics," in *Essays Philosophical and Theological*, trans. J. C. G. Greig (London, 1955); Hans- Georg Gadamer, *Wahrheit und Methode*, 3rd ed., (Tübingen, 1972).

17. *Being and Time*, p. 195.

18. See the remarks of Hirsch on genre and preunderstanding, *Validity in Interpretation*, especially pp. 76 ff.

Style as Interpretation

1. René Wellek finds fault with Auerbach's *Mimesis* for confusing two kinds of reality, social and "existential." I do not quite see the force of this objection since the reality perceived in crisis has no significance except as it emerges from a world in which social reality stands in contrast to it. See *Concepts of Criticism* (New Haven, 1963), p. 236.

2. See Erich Kahler, *The Inward Turn of Narrative*, trans, R. and C. Winston (Princeton, 1973).

3. We have a superb review and evaluation of Auerbach's work by Arthur R. Evans, "Erich Auerbach as European Critic," *Romance Philology* 25, no. 2 (November 1971): 193–215. I am greatly indebted to this article for bringing Auerbach's numerous studies to so sharp a focus. The most important of Auerbach's studies dealing with the literary interpretation of reality are *Dante als Dichter der Irdischen Welt* (Berlin and Leipzig, 1929; E. T.: *Dante: Poet of the Secular World* [Chicago, 1961]); *Mimesis: The Representation of Reality in Western Literature*, trans. W. R. Trask (Princeton, 1953); and his famous essay "Figura," translated by Ralph Manheim in *Scenes from the Drama of European Literature* (New York, 1959), pp. 11–76.

4. *Dante als Dichter*, p. 166 f., E. T. p. 133. This theme occurs frequently in Auerbach's work but is theoretically developed in his *Typologische Motive in der mittelalterlichen Literatur* (Cologne, 1953; new ed. 1964). See Evans' comments on this citation in his article.

5. The term allegory among Romantic thinkers was used in both a positive and a negative way. Coleridge made a famous distinction between "allegory" and "symbolism" to the disadvantage of the former. Schelling's use of the concept of allegory in reference to Dante means to refer to the universal significance which Dante can confer on the historically and uniquely rendered

individual. Schelling's essay is available in Hugo Friedrich, ed., *Dante Alighieri, Aufsätze zur "Divina Commedia"* (Darmstadt, 1968).

6. Part III, chap. 3. I cite the excellent translation of this passage made by Evans in "Erich Auerbach as European Critic," p. 200.

7. *Dante als Dichter*, p. 22 f.; E. T. p. 14 f.

8. The conceptions of type and antitype are not always in an inverse relationship. Sometimes "type" is used as equivalent to "antitype," and sometimes the reverse is true. It is thus legitimate to speak of Christ as either a type or antitype of Adam. Modern use of this terminology tends to confer on the concepts a kind of precision they do not have in the New Testament. See the entries and references in Bauer-Arndt-Gingrich, *A Greek-English Lexicon of the New Testament* (Chicago, 1957).

9. Cf. the first essay and the excursus in Auerbach's *Literatursprache und Publikum*, 1958, trans. Ralph Manheim, *Literary Language and its Public in Late Antiquity and in the Middle Ages* (New York, 1965).

10. Auerbach was a historical scholar, but the validity of theological ways of reading the Bible even in a thoroughly secularized and literary-critical context is interestingly advanced by Northrop Frye, *The Anatomy of Criticism* (Princeton, 1957), p. 314.

11. See, for example, the treatment of St. John and St. Paul in Rudolf Bultmann's *Theology of the New Testament*.

12. "Headbands spattered with venom, black and foul, his hands strain in the effort to tear apart their knots, he shouts terrible cries to heaven, just as the bellowing bull when he rushes from the altar, the axe still wavering in the wound of his neck."

13. See, for example, Thorleif Boman, *Das hebräische Denken im Vergleich mit dem griechischen*, 4th ed. (Göttingen, 1965). Only the third edition of this book is available in English, and that does not contain Boman's reply to various critics, especially James Barr, concerning his method of discovering biblical "thought forms" through a lexicographical study of the biblical languages.

New Wine in Old Bottles

1. Karl Jaspers, "Myth and Religion," in *Kerygma and Myth* 2, ed. Hans-Werner Bartsch, trans. Reginald Fuller (London, 1962), p. 157. This volume is available with *Kerygma and Myth* 1, 2nd ed. 1964 (1st ed. 1953) bound together as *Kerygma and Myth: A Theological Debate* (London, 1972).

2. Excellent accounts of biblical exegesis can be found in *The Cambridge History of the Bible*, vols. 1 and 2. A classic historical study is F. W. Farrar, *History of Interpretation* (London, 1886). A lucid modern account is R.M. Grant, *A Short History of the Interpretation of the Bible* (London, 1965). A valuable but more specialized study is J. S. Preus, *From Shadow to Promise: Old Testament Interpretation from Augustine to Luther* (Cambridge, Mass., 1969). Although the Reformers generally discarded allegorism of the conventional sort and postulated that *Scriptura Scripturae interpres,* they by no

means abandoned prophetic typological exegesis. For the patristic and medieval periods, the following are most useful: H. A. Wolfson, *Philo: Foundations of Religious Philosophy in Judaism, Christianity and Islam,* 2 vols., 2nd ed. (Cambridge, Mass., 1948); Beryl Smalley, *The Study of the Bible in the Middle Ages,* 2nd ed. (Oxford, 1952; Notre Dame, Ind., 1964); Henri de Lubac, *Exegèse médiévale: les quattre sens de l'Ecriture,* 4 vols.(Paris, 1959–1964). For studies of allegory in literature Dante scholarship takes first place. We now possess the excellent study of Robert B Hollander, Jr., *Allegory in Dante's Commedia* Princeton, 1969). Hollander reviews and evaluates the literature on Dante's allegorism and offers his own penetrating solutions to some of the outstanding problems. For a study of allegory as a general critical and literary concept see Angus Fletcher, *Allegory: The Theory of the Symbolic Mode* (Ithaca, 1964). See also the earlier study by Edwin Honig, *Dark Conceit: The Making of Allegory* (Evanston, Ill., 1959).

3. XV, ix, 15. The traditional definition of allegory was sometimes taken to apply to the New Testament parables. While to some extent the parables may be so read, they are certainly not systematic allegories and are not generally concerned with matters of a theoretical or technically theological character. The parable is essentially an illustrative tale working through similitudes, and the exegesis it demands is rarely of an explicitly allegorical kind. For a comprehensive discussion of this problem see Dan Otto Via, Jr., *The Parables: Their Literary and Existential Dimension* (Philadelphia, 1967).

4. Some confusion as I noted before may arise from the actual use of the terms type and antitype in Scripture and in early Christian literature. Although antitype may imply at times a negative kind of relation to its type, it may simply be a synonym of type. Thus, we may have a type referring to an earlier type or an antitype referring to its earlier type and mean simply the same relationship. See the entries on type and antitype, Bauer-Arndt-Gingrich, *A Greek Lexicon of the New Testament* (Chicago, 1957). Both type and antitype can either mean original or copy so that both terms may be ambiguous.

5. A comprehensive account of the senses of Scripture by St. Thomas is found in no. 7 of the *Questions Quodlibetales, Questiones Disputatae et Quodlibetales* III, cura et studio R. Spiazzi, (*Opera Omnia* in the Leonine edition).

In *Quodlibet* VII, Q. vi., Art. 16, Ad 3, Responsio, St. Thomas says: "Sicut enim homo potest adhibere ad aliquid significandum aliquas voces vel aliquas similitudines fictas: ita deus adhibet ad significationem aliquorum ipsum cursum rerum suae providentiae subjectarum. Significare autem aliquid per verba vel per similitudines fictas ad significandum tantum ordinatas: non facit nisi sensum literalem."

6. There is a new edition and French translation of Heraclitus: Héraclite, *Allégories d'Homère,* Greek text and French translation, edited by Félix Buffière (Paris, 1962). The edition supersedes that of F. Oelmann, *Questiones Homericae* (Leipzig, 1910).

7. See Werner Jaeger, *Theology of the Early Greek Philosophers* (Oxford, 1947), pp. 50 ff. and his *Early Christianity and Greek Paideia* (Cambridge, Mass., 1961), pp. 127 ff.

8. On Philo, see especially Irmgaard Christiansen, *Die Technik der allegorischen Auslegungswissenschaft bei Philon von Alexandrien* (Tübingen,

1969), and on Marcion, the classic study of Adolf von Harnack, *Marcion: Das Evangelium vom Fremden Gott,* 2nd ed. (Leipzig, 1924). Cf. the comments of Jaeger, *Early Christianity,* pp. 48 ff.

9. Buffière, *Allégories d'Homère,* 5, 2.

10. Heraclitus, *Allegories,* 3, 2 and Buffière, n. 6, p. 90.

11. Heraclitus, *Allegories,* 4, and Jaeger, *Early Christianity,* pp. 127–28.

12. Jaeger, *Early Christianity,* p. 128.

13. Hans Jonas, *The Gnostic Religion: The Message of the Alien God and the Beginnings of Christianity,* 2nd ed. (Boston, 1963), p. 92.

14. Northrop Frye, *Anatomy of Criticism* (Princeton, 1957), pp. 89–90. Cf. the author's remarks, again identifying allegory with commentary, on pp. 341–42: "Commentary, we remember, is allegorization, and any great work of literature may carry an infinite amount of commentary. . . . Commentary which has no sense of the archetypal shape of literature as a whole, then, continues the tradition of allegorized myth, and inherits its characteristics of brilliance, ingenuity, and futility. . . . The only cure for this situation is the supplementing of allegorical with archetypal criticism."

15. Frye does, in passing, acknowledge the existence of "genuine allegory" but does not very clearly tell us what that would be if all commentary is allegory: "Genuine allegory is a structural element in literature: it has to be there, and cannot be added by critical interpretation alone." *Anatomy of Criticism,* p. 54.

16. A brilliant discussion of these problems of interpretation is to be found in E. D. Hirsch, *Validity in Interpretation* (New Haven, 1967). His critique of Hans-Georg Gadamer's *Wahrheit und Methode: Grundzüge einer philosophischen Hermeneutik,* 3rd ed. (Tübingen, 1972) is particularly acute. Gadamer, following Heidegger and to some degree Bultmann, is profoundly concerned with the way in which historicity affects understanding, but is completely sceptical concerning the recovery of authorial intention or even the importance of doing so. Hirsch, distinguishing between meaning and significance, defends interpretation from the outcome of simply making the text mean whatever the interpreter wants it to mean, a practice sometimes defended as giving us the "existentialistic" reference of the text. Hirsch follows the hermeneutical theories of Emilio Betti. See Betti's *Teoria generale della interpretazione,* 2 vols. (Milan, 1955) and *Die Hermeneutik als allgemeine Methodik der Geisteswissenschaften* (Tübingen, 1962).

A new work by E. D. Hirsch, Jr., *The Aims of Interpretation* (Chicago, 1976), appeared after my manuscript was complete. In it Professor Hirsch elaborates the distinction between meaning and significance advanced in his earlier work, deepens his view of interpretation as having the value of "application," vigorously exposes the weaknesses in the arguments of historical, psychological, and linguistic relativists and, most gratifyingly, attacks the assumption that what is aesthetically excellent and what is humanly beneficial must be without hesitation conceived of as united.

17. See the remarks of Hirsch, *Validity,* p. 112 and Appendix II, "Gadamer's Theory of Interpretation," pp. 245–64.

18. Various parts of Scripture are still occasionally regarded as constructed allegories. The passages in question are usually to be found in Ezekiel or Daniel and are clearly apocalyptic in character. Apocalyptic literature is essentially prophetic myth, and while it lends itself to allegorical uncoding,

it is essentially predictive in function. The "Son of Man" is not an allegorical figure but a concrete heavenly being who will appear at the end-time. If the beast of the Apocalypse is Vespasian, *Nero redivivus,* what we have is a typological, mythical figure, the beast who "incarnates" himself in one persecuting emperor or another. In St. John's visions, the other world and the fulfillment of prophecy are grasped as imagery.

19. If this mode of allegorism led to a sharp distinction between esoteric and exoteric meanings and reserved the pure truth for an intellectual elite, it also led to various theories of accommodative metaphor. God used figurative and symbolic expressions in Scripture to express something of himself in a mode that everyone might understand. St. Thomas gives classic expression to this doctrine and it finds its way into the poetic conceptions of Dante and Milton. See my *Structure and Thought in Paradiso* (Ithaca, 1958), especially the chapter on Dante's conception of poetic expression.

20. Robert Neville, "Specialities and Worlds," *The Hastings Center Studies* 2, no. 1 (January 1974): 60.

21. Many of the Freudian interpreters of humanistic texts as well as the French structuralists and their American disciples have returned to what is essentially a system of allegorical interpretation as "application." History is annihilated along with authorial intention; each text is treated as a specimen of the universal text; the fragments of texts, i.e., units yielded by analysis, are arranged into patterns of one kind or another and thus generally yield the sort of meaning the exegete wishes to find.

What Clifford Geertz has to say about Lévi-Strauss can be applied with little change to the way structuralists often deal with literature ("The Cerebral Savage: On the Work of Claude Lévi-Strauss," *The Interpretation of Cultures* [New York, 1973], pp. 345–59): "With this door open [binary opposition] all things are possible . . . any classificatory scheme can be exposed . . . they always trace down to an underlying opposition of paired terms . . . " (p. 354). Geertz summarizes as follows: "For what Lévi-Strauss has made for himself is an infernal culture machine. It annuls history, reduces sentiment to a shadow of the intellect, and replaces the particular minds of particular savages with the Savage Mind immanent in us all" (p. 355).

A recent comprehensive study of structuralism in literary criticism is Jonathan Culler, *Structuralist Poetics: Structuralism, Linguistics and the Study of Literature* (London, 1975). The author is attentive to the limitations of structuralism but less mindful of the limitations of linguistics as applied to criticism. Whether the concept of "linguistic competence" can be transformed directly into a notion of "literary competence" is doubtful. It seems to me that Culler excessively simplifies the nature of understanding, the complexity of the act of reading, and the truly central problems of the nature of truth and language. See the long and brilliant review of this book by Paul Bové in *Boundary 2,* vol. 5, (1976): 263–84, "The Poetics of Coercion: An Interpretation of Literary Competence."

Robert Scholes in *Structuralism in Literature: An Introduction* (New Haven, 1974) does what he claims to do, introduces the subject. This work closes with a paean to the "structuralist imagination" and with great expectations from structuralism as a new system of belief. I leave the reader to judge for himself how redemptive or illuminating structuralism will prove itself to be concerning politics (p. 193) and even, to my surprise, love (p. 197).

The Platonic Debate over Myth, Truth, and Virtue

1. G. S. Kirk, *Myth: Its Meaning and Function in Ancient and Other Cultures* (Cambridge, 1970), p. 250.

2. For an extensive discussion of medieval views of metaphor especially as they apply to Dante, see my *Structure and Thought in the Paradiso* (Ithaca, 1958), chap. 2, "Dante's Conception of Poetic Expressions"; cf. Aquinas, *Scriptum super libros sententiarum Magistri Petri Lombardi*, Prolog. Q. 1, Art. 5, ad 3, Pierre Mandonnet, ed., vol. 1 (Paris, 1929), p. 18: "Ad tertium dicendum, quod poetica scientia est de his quae propter defectum veritatis non possunt a ratione capi: unde oportet quod quasi quibusdam similitudinibus ratio seducatur: theologia autem est de his quae sunt supra rationem: et ideo modus symbolicus utrique communis est, cum neutra rationi proportionetur."

3. The classic source for understanding this debate occurs in Origen's polemic against Celsus. See *Origen Contra Celsum*, trans. with introduction and notes by Henry Chadwick (Cambridge, 1953).

4. On the Platonic tradition of poetic theology see J. A. Stewart, *The Myths of Plato*, ed. G. R. Levy, (London, 1960): D. C. Allen, *Mysteriously Meant: The Rediscovery of Pagan Symbolism and Allegorical Interpretation in the Renaissance* (Baltimore and London, 1970); D. P. Walker, *The Ancient Theology: Studies in Christian Platonism from the Fifteenth to the Eighteenth Centuries* (London, 1972). With special reference to the visual arts, see Edgar Wind, *Pagan Mysteries of the Renaissance* (London, 1958). For a fascinating study of the emergence of the scientific study of mythology, see F. E. Manuel, *The Eighteenth Century Confronts the Gods*, (Cambridge, Mass., 1959).

5. Wind, *Pagan Mysteries*, p. 167.

6. On universalism and the concept of symbolic thought in the Renaissance see the study of Ernst Cassirer, "Giovanni Pico Della Mirandola: A Study in the History of Renaissance Ideas," in *Renaissance Essays*, ed. P. O. Kristeller and P. P. Wiener (New York, 1968), pp. 11–60. This article was originally published in *Journal of the History of Ideas* 3, no. 2 (1942). See also the penetrating observations on Renaissance neoplatonism of Erwin Panofsky, *Renaissance and Renascences in Western Art* (Stockholm, 1960), pp. 182 ff.

7. The great debate inaugurated by Bultmann has inspired a considerable literature. The essential texts, including Jaspers' critique, are available for the English reader in *Kerygma and Myth: A Theological Debate*, ed. Hans Werner Bartsch, trans. Reginald Fuller (London, 1972). For attempts to go beyond Bultmann's exegetical methods see J. M. Robinson and J. E. Cobb, Jr., eds., *The New Hermeneutic* (New York, 1964). For some of the more recent literature on the "two-culture" debate inaugurated by C. P. Snow, see Martin Green, *Science and the Shabby Curate of Poetry* (London, 1964); Sir Peter Medawar, "Science and Literature," *Perspectives in Biology and Medicine* 12, no. 4 (Summer, 1969): 529–46; J. H. Plumb, ed., *Crisis in the Humanities* (Penguin Books, 1964). For a discussion of this problem in the light of its historical background I refer the reader to my *Renaissance and Revolution: The Remaking of European Thought* (New York, 1965), chap. 6.

8. Yehezekel Kaufmann, *The Religion of Israel*, trans. and abridged by Moshe Greenberg (London, 1961), pp. 71–72.

9. For a classic study of the affirmative side of the Platonic view of myth see J. A. Stewart, *The Myths of Plato,* ed. G. R. Levy (London, 1960), a work originally published in 1904. See also Friedrich Solmsen's *Plato's Theology* (Ithaca, 1942).

10. A. N. Whitehead in *The Philosophical Review* 46: 182–83, cited in A. H. Johnson, ed., *The Wit and Wsdom of Alfred North Whitehead* (Boston, 1947), p. 50.

11. Rudolph Bultmann, *Primitive Christianity in Its Contemporary Setting,* trans. R. H. Fuller (New York, 1956), p. 125.

12. Kirk, *Myth,* p. 259.

13. Kirk (*Myth,* p. 250) favors the Platonic use of myth when compared to what the Alexandrians made of it! "When rationalism, working with special force through the Sophists, had finally undermined belief in the mythical world of the past—at least among the educated classes—the dominion by myth of the forms of literature became sterile and restrictive, and the whole delicately balanced system collapsed. Plato, although he abused the poets, temporarily reasserted the role of myth in his own practice; but it was not long before the Alexandrians discovered for myths a new and wholly artificial, and therefore destructive, role."

14. For a brief but very penetrating description of the present state of studies in mythology see Robert Ackerman's review article, "Writing about Writing about Myth," *Journal of the History of Ideas* no. 1 (January-March, 1973): 147–55. A good final statement of Jung's views may be conveniently found in his quasi-autobiography, *Memories, Dreams and Reflections,* trans. Richard and Clara Winston (London, 1963), especially chaps 9 and 10. Cassirer's view of myth is in vol. 2 of his *The Philosophy of Symbolic Forms,* trans. Ralph Manheim (New Haven, 1955).

15. (New York, 1929), p. 19.

16. J. J. Bachofen, *Der Mythos von Orient und Okzident* (Munich, 1926) cited in *Kerygma and Myth,* 1, p. 159. Cf. the remarks of Joseph Campbell in his introduction to *Myth, Religion and Mother Right: Selected Writings of J. J. Bachofen,* trans. Ralph Mannheim (Princeton, 1967), pp. xlv ff.

17. On the distinction between canonical and apocryphal myth see Northrop Frye, *The Anatomy of Criticism,* pp. 54 ff. and 126 ff. Cf., e.g., "Again, nearly every civilization has, in its stock of traditional myths, a particular group which is thought of as more serious, more authoritative, more educational and closer to fact and truth than the rest. For most poets of the Christian era who have used both the Bible and Classical literature, the latter has not stood on the same plane of authority as the former, although they are equally mythological as far as literary criticism is concerned. This distinction of canonical and apocryphal myth, which can be found even in primitive societies, gives to the former groups a particular thematic importance [p. 54]. . . . each mode of literature projects its own existential projection. So mythology projects itself as theology in that a mythopoeic poet accepts some myths as 'true' and shapes his poetic structure accordingly" (p. 64).

18. For an extensive study of the exegetical background to Milton's use of both Christian and classical allusion see William G. Madsen, *From Shadowy Types to Truth: Studies in Milton's Symbolism* (New Haven, 1968). See also A. C. Charity, *Events and Their Afterlife: The Dialectics of Christian Typology in the Bible and Dante,* (Cambridge, 1966). The classic study of Jean

Seznec is still of great value, *The Survival of the Pagan Gods: The Mythologi-cal Tradition and Its Place in Renaissance Humanism and Art,* trans. B. F. Sessions (New York, 1953). Two interesting studies by modern theologians of the relation between pagan and Christian myth are Jean Daniélou, *Mythes paiens, mystère chrétien (Paris, 1966),* and Hugo Rahner, *Greek Myths and Christian Mystery,* trans. Brian Battershaw (London, 1963).

19. The best treatment of the Freudian theory of symbolism is Ernest Jones, "The Theory of Symbolism," *Papers in Psychoanalysis,* 5th ed. (1948, repr. New York, 1961). See also for some divergent views, David Rapaport, trans. and ed., *Organization and Pathology of Thought: Selected Sources* (New York, 1951), Pt. III, "Symbolism." See also the recent study of Paul Ricoeur, *Freud and Philosophy: An Essay in Interpretation,* trans. D. Savage (New Haven, 1970). This lengthy study of Freud discusses in part one, the problem of the twofold character of hermeneutics: (1) as the process of dimin-ishing illusion; (2) as the explication of meanings, and the expanding of the significance of a text. There is throughout the book a substantial treatment of the psychoanalytic theory of symbolism with an attempt to define its uses and limitations. Where Jones distinguishes between the symbolic and metaphori-cal processes, Ricoeur seems, at times, to distinguish between an "archeol-ogy" of the mind and its "teleology"; that is to say that Ricoeur ac-knowledges the task of demythologizing thought but parallels this necessity with the important task of remythologizing thought.

20. Sigmund Freud, *Moses and Monotheism,* trans. Katherine Jones (New York, 1939), pp. 51–52.

Interpretation, Humanistic Culture, and Cultural Change

1. E.g. see C. D. Darlington, *The Evolution of Man and Society* (London, 1965).

2. Cf. the thesis of Elizabeth Sewell's book, *The Orphic Voice: Poetry and Natural History* (New Haven, 1960).

3. See the study of Robert L. Heilbroner, *An Inquiry into the Human Prospect* (New York, 1974). This pessimistic thesis on the future of mankind has often been attacked without being refuted. If the trends we now discern continue we are headed for great social upheavals. The power, authority, and coercion needed to stabilize the world in such circumstances will be greater than any that men have known hitherto. The very process of forestalling the dangers inherent in the present form occurring in the future will change the political order of things so as to diminish freedom and often eliminate it. That this might happen is scarcely refutable if the seeds of the future are germinat-ing now.

4. For a brilliantly drawn set of contrasts between biological and cultural change see the Nobel speech of Konrad Lorenz, "Analogy as a Source of Knowledge," *Science,* 185 (19 July 1974); 229–34. I have drawn heavily from the work of Lorenz for what I have to say on this subject. For the use of metaphors of organic growth and of life cycles in theories of social develop-

ment from antiquity to the present see R. A. Nisbet, *Social Change and History: Aspects of the Western Theory of Development* (New York, 1969).

5. See the interesting and suggestive reflections of Denis de Rougement "The Responsibility of the Writer in Present-Day European Society," trans. Guy Daniels, *The American Pen*, Spring, 1974, pp. 12–26. The author's well-known tendency to large, brilliant, and somewhat misleading generalizations makes him read back into the thirteenth century a cultural situation which seems to me to be distinctively modern: "From the *Bhagavad Gita* to the *Quest for the Grail*, from the tragedy of Oedipus to that of Tristan, all the great works of world literature up to the 12th century were born and lived in symbiosis with the community. They expressed its finalities, its ground rules and its misadventures." He adds that after this period, literature became a "solitary song of the heart," Catholic dogma replaced myth as the agency of religious and social cohesion, and the national state took over the function of arranging and adjudicating human relationships. He is certainly correct about the increasing demythologization and secularization of culture, but are the works of Dante, Shakespeare, Cervantes, Montaigne, etc., to be described as examples of a "solitary song of the heart"? See pp. 14 ff.

6. Ibid., p. 13. As his translator, Guy Daniels points out, *gueuloir* is a word coined by Flaubert from the French word for mouth or throat to suggest a testing place for his rhythms.

7. Lionel Trilling, "On the Teaching of Modern Literature," *Beyond Culture: Essays on Literature and Learning* (New York, 1965), p. 3. Cf. Hans Küng, *On Being a Christian*, trans. Edward Quinn (London, 1977), p. 38: "in view of this situation [the crisis of secular humanism], after so many disappointments, a certain scepticism in regard to humanism is understandable. Many secular analysts today frequently restrict their work in philosophy, linguistics, ethnology, sociology, individual and social psychology to making sense out of the illogical, confused, contradictory and unintelligible material by not attempting to give it any meaning at all, but by proceeding as in the natural sciences to establish the positive data (Positivism) and the formal structures (Structuralism) and being satisfied with measuring, calculating, controlling, programming and prognosticating the individual sequences."

Myth and Science in the Theology of Rudolf Bultmann

1. Bultmann's views on myth and those of his critics and supporters may be found in *Kerygma and Myth: A Theological Debate*, ed. Hans-Werner Bartsch and trans. Reginald Fuller (London, 1972), which contains the only two volumes of the series yet to have appeared in English. His views are also briefly and lucidly stated in *Jesus Christ and Mythology* (New York, 1958). His important essay "The Problem of Hermeneutics" can be found in *Essays Philosophical and Theological*, trans. J. C. G. Greig (London and New York, 1955). Various studies of Bultmann's theology have appeared. The one I have found most useful is Walter Schmithals, *An Introduction to the Theology of Rudolf Bultmann*, trans. John Bowden (London, 1968).

2. *Kerygma and Myth* 1, p. 22 f.

3. Jaspers, *Kerygma and Myth* 2, pp. 133 ff.

4. Jaspers, *Kerygma and Myth* 1, pp. 143–144.

5. Bultmann's penetrating observations concerning the contrast between both the scientific and mythological and the hellenic and Hebraic views of the world are available in his *Primitive Christianity in Its Contemporary Setting,* trans. R. H. Fuller (New York, 1956).

6. Bultmann, *Kerygma and Myth* 1, p. 14.

7. Harnack, *What is Christianity?* (New York, 1957) pp. 14–15.

8. Harnack, *What is Christianity?* pp. 300–301.

9. Bultmann's remarks on religion and its purpose may be found, e.g., in *Kerygma and Myth* 1, pp. 12–13.

10. See the remarks on the history of the concept of myth in regard to the Bible in Schmithals, *An Introduction,* pp. 260 ff. Frank Manuel's *The Eighteenth Century Confronts the Gods* (Cambridge, Mass., 1959) is indispensable for the early history of the scientific study of myth.

11. Bultmann, *Jesus Christ and Mythology,* p. 20.

12. Bultmann, according to Schmithals, *Introduction,* pp. 303 ff.

13. See Bultmann's remarkable commentary on St. John's Gospel, *The Gospel of John,* trans. G. R. Beasley-Murray (Oxford, 1971). This has been called the greatest commentary on any book of the Bible ever written. One should compare the less philosophically interpreted study of C. H. Dodd, *The Interpretation of the Fourth Gospel* (Cambridge, 1953).

14. Bultmann, *Kerygma and Myth* 1, pp. 15–16, 13.

15. Bultmann, *Kerygma and Myth* 1, p. 608.

16. Paul Tillich, *Dynamics of Faith* (New York, 1957), p. 51. Cf. the critique of Bultmann's mythological views in John Macquarrie, *The Scope of Demythologizing: Bultmann and His Critics* (London and New York, 1960). Macquarrie argues that theology is the phenomenology of faith and that it prescinds from any correspondence theory of its truth. The validity of any statements about religion comes from the analysis of religious experience. Its truth, like Heidegger's conception of truth, lies in "unconcealing" what we are talking about. See especially pp. 202 ff.

17. *Jesus Christ and Mythology,* p. 65.

18. Ibid., pp. 64–72.

19. Ibid., p. 84.

20. Ibid., p. 85.

21. Ibid., p. 40.

Bibliography

1. General Theory of Interpretation

Betti, Emilio. *Teoria generale della interpretazione.* 2 vols. Milan, 1955.
——. *Die Hermeneutik als allgemeine Methodik der Geisteswissenshaften.* Tübingen, 1962.
Boeckh, August. *Encyclopädie und Methodologie der philologischen Wissenschaften.* 2nd ed. Leipzig, 1886.
Dilthey, Wilhelm. "Die Entstehung der Hermeneutik," *Gesammelte Schriften* 5. Leipzig and Berlin, 1924.
——. "Die Entstehung der Hermeneutik," *Gesammelte Schriften* 5. Edited by Georg Misch. 2nd ed. Stuttgart and Göttingen, 1957.
——. *Pattern and Meaning in History.* Translated and edited by H. P. Rickman. New York, 1962.
Ehrlich, W. *Das Verstehen. Zurich and Leipzig, 1939.*
Gadamer, Hans-Georg. *Wahrheit und Methode: Grundzüge einer philosophischen Hermeneutik.* 3rd ed. Tübingen, 1972. E. T., *Truth and Method.* Translated by G. Barden and J. Cumming, from 2nd ed. London, 1975.
Hirsch, E. D. *Validity in Interpretation.* New Haven, 1967.
——. *The Aims of Interpretation.* Chicago, 1976.
Hodges, H. A. *Wilhelm Dilthey: An Introduction.* London, 1944.
Palmer, Richard E. *Hermeneutics: Interpretive Theory in Schleiermacher, Dilthey, Heidegger, and Gadamer.* Evanston, Ill., 1969.

Schleiermacher, Fr. D. E. *Hermeneutik*. Edited by Heinz Kimmerle. Heidelberg, 1959.

Wach, Joachim. *Das Verstehen: Grundzuge einer Geschichte der hermeneutischen Theorie im 19. Jahrhundert*. 3 vols. Tübingen, 1926–33.

2. Language and Philosophy

Black, Max. *Models and Metaphors: Studies in Language and Philosophy*. New York, 1962.

Cassirer, Ernst. *The Philosophy of Symbolic Forms,* vol. 1: *Language*. Translated by Ralph Manheim. New Haven, 1953.

———. *The Philosophy of Symbolic Forms,* vol. 2: *Mythical Thought*. Translated by Ralph Manheim. New Haven, 1955.

———. *The Philosophy of Symbolic Forms,* vol. 3: *The Phenomenology of Knowledge*. Translated by Ralph Manheim. New Haven, 1957.

———. *The Logic of the Humanities*. Translated by C. S. Howe. New Haven, 1960.

Chomsky, Noam. *Language and Mind*. New York, 1968.

Daniélou, Jean. "The Problem of Symbolism," *Thought* 25 (1950): 423–440.

Geertz, Clifford. *The Interpretation of Cultures*. New York, 1973.

Heidegger, Martin. *Unterwegs zur Sprache*. Pfullingen, 1959.

———. *Being and Time*. Translated by John Macquarrie and Edward Robinson. New York, 1962.

Lane, Michael, ed. *Introduction to Structuralism*. New York, 1970.

Langer, Susanne K. *Philosophy in a New Key: A Study in the Symbolism of Reason, Rite, and Art*. 3rd ed. Cambridge, Mass., 1957.

Leach, Edmund. *Lévi-Strauss*. London, 1970.

Lenneberg. E. H. *Biological Foundations of Language*. New York, 1967.

Lévi-Strauss, Claude. *Structural Anthropology*. Translated by C. Jacobson and B. G. Schoepf. New York, 1963.

Lloyd, G. E. R. *Polarity and Analogy*. Cambridge, 1966.

Merleau-Ponty, Maurice. *The Primacy of Perception and Other Essays*. Translated by James M. Edie. Evanston, Ill., 1964.

Morris, Charles. *Signs, Language and Behavior*. New York, 1946.

Piaget, Jean. *Structuralism*. Translated and edited by Chaninah Maschler. London, 1971.

Rose, C. Brooke. *A Grammar of Metaphor*. New York, 1958.

Ryle, Gilbert. "The Theory of Meaning." In *British Philosophy in the Mid-Century,* edited by C. A. Mace. London, 1957. Also in *The Importance of Language,* edited by Max Black. Englewood Cliffs, N.J., 1962.

Saussure, Ferdinand de. *Course in General Linguistics*. Edited by C. Bally and A. Sechehaye. Translated by W. Baskin. New York, 1959.

Shibles, W. A. *An Analysis of Metaphor in the Light of W. M. Urban's Theories*. The Hague, 1971.

Stenson, Sten H. *Sense and Nonsense in Religion: An Essay on the Language and Phenomenology of Religion.* New York, 1969.

Urban, Wilbur M. *Language and Reality: The Philosophy of Language and the Principles of Symbolism.* London, 1939.

Wheelwright, Philip. *Metaphor and Reality.* Bloomington, Ind., 1962.

Whitehead, A. N. *Symbolism: Its Meaning and Effect.* New York, 1927.

Wittgenstein, Ludwig. *Philosophical Investigations.* Translated by G. E. M. Anscombe. New York, 1963.

3. Classical Allegorism and Mythology: The Classical Tradition

Allen, D. C. *Mysteriously Meant: The Rediscovery of Pagan Symbolism and Allegorical Interpretation in the Renaissance.* Baltimore, 1970.

Bachofen, J. J. *Myth, Religion and Mother Right: Selected Writings of J. J. Bachofen.* Translated by Ralph Manheim. Princeton, 1967.

Buffière, Félix. *Les myths d'Homère et la pensée grecque.* Paris, 1956.

Cassirer, Ernst. "Giovanni Pico Della Mirandola: A Study in the History of Renaissance Ideas." In *Renaissance Essays,* edited by P. O. Kristeller and P. P. Wiener, pp. 11–60. New York, 1968.

Daniélou, Jean. *Myths paiens, mystère chrétien.* Paris, 1966.

Decharme, P. *La Critique des traditions religieuses chez les Grecs.* Paris, 1904.

Frutiger, P. *Les mythes de Platon.* Paris, 1930.

Héraclite. *Allégories d'Homère.* Greek text and French translation by Félix Buffière. Paris, 1962.

Heracliti Questiones Homericae. Edited by F. Oelmann. Leipzig, 1910.

Jaeger, Werner. *Theology of the Early Greek Philosophers.* Oxford, 1947.

———. *Early Christianity and Greek Paideia.* Cambridge, Mass., 1951.

Kirk, G. S. *Myth: Its Meaning and Functions in Ancient and Other Cultures.* Cambridge, 1970.

Manuel, Frank E. *The Eighteenth Century Confronts the Gods.* Cambridge, Mass., 1959.

Panofsky, Erwin. *Renaissance and Renascences in Western Art.* Stockholm, 1960.

Pepin, Jean. *Mythe et allegorie: Les origines grecques et les contestations Judeo-Chrétiennes.* Paris, 1958.

Rahner, Hugo. *Greek Myths and Christian Mystery.* Translated by Brian Battershaw. London, 1963. Reprint New York, 1971.

Seznec, Jean. *The Survival of the Pagan Gods: The Mythological Tradition and Its Place in Renaissance Humanism and Art.* Translated by B. F. Sessions. New York, 1953.

Solmsen, Friedrich. *Plato's Theology.* Ithaca, 1942.

Stewart, J. A. *The Myths of Plato.* Edited by G. R. Levy. London, 1960.

Tate, J. "The Beginnings of Greek Allegory," *Classical Review* 41 (1927): 214–15.

———. "Plato and Allegorical Interpretation," *The Classical Quarterly* 23 (1929): 142–154, and 24 (1930): 1–10.

———. "On the History of Allegorism," *The Classical Quarterly* 28 (1934): 105–114.

Walker, D. P. *The Ancient Theology: Studies in Christian Platonism from the Fifteenth to the Eighteenth Century.* London, 1972.

Wehrli, F. *Zur Geschichte der Allegorischten Deutung Homers in Altertum.* Leipzig, 1928.

Wind, Edgar. *Pagan Mysteries of the Renaissance.* London, 1958.

4. Biblical Interpretation

The Cambridge History of the Bible, vol. 1: *From the Beginnings to Jerome.* Edited by P. R. Ackroyd and C. F. Evans. Cambridge, 1970. Especially Part IV, chap. 12, "The Interpretation of the Old Testament in the New," and Part V: "The Bible in the Early Church."

The Cambridge History of the Bible, vol. 2: *The West from the Fathers to the Reformation.* Edited by G. W. H. Lampe. Cambridge, 1969. See especially Part VI: "The Exposition and Exegesis of Scripture."

The Cambridge History of the Bible, vol. 3: *The West from the Reformation to the Present Day.* Edited by S. L. Greenslade. Cambridge, 1963.

Achtemeier, Paul J. *An Introduction to the New Hermeneutic.* Philadelphia, 1969.

Augustine, St. *On Christian Doctrine.* Translated by D. W. Robertson, Jr. New York, 1958.

Barr, J. D. *The Semantics of Biblical Language.* Oxford, 1961.

———. *The Bible in the Modern World.* London, 1973.

Bartsch, Hans-Werner. "Bultmann and Jaspers." In *Kerygma and Myth* 2. London, 1962.

Beardslee. William A. *Literary Criticism of the New Testament.* Philadelphia, 1970.

Bercovitch, Sacvan. "Selective Check-List on Typology," *Early American Literature* 5, no. 1, pt. 2 (Spring, 1970), pp. 1–76.

Blackman, E. C. *Biblical Interpretation.* Philadelphia, 1957.

Boman, Thorleif. *Hebrew Thought Compared with Greek.* Translated by L. Moreau. London, 1960.

Brøndsted, Gustav. "Two World-Concepts—Two Languages." In *Kerygma and Myth* 2. London, 1962.

Bultmann, Rudolf. *Theology of the New Testament.* 2 vols. London, 1952 and 1955.

———. "The Problem of Hermeneutics," *Essays Philosophical and Theo-*

logical. Translated by J. C. G. Greig. London and New York, 1955. (*Glauben und Verstehen,* vol. 2, 3rd ed., 1961).

————. *History and Eschatology.* Edinburgh, 1957.

————. *Jesus Christ and Mythology.* New York, 1958.

————. "The Case for Demythologizing." In *Kerygma and Myth* 2. London, 1962.

————. "New Testament and Mythology." In *Kerygma and Myth* 1. 2nd ed. London, 1964.

Christiansen, Irmgaard. *Die Technik der allegorischen Auslegungswissenschaft bei Philon von Alexandrien.* Tübingen, 1969.

Daniélou, Jean. *Sacramentum futuri: Etudes sur les origines de la typologie biblique.* Paris, 1950. E. T., Westminster, Md., 1960.

Farrar, F. W. *History of Interpretation.* London, 1886.

Farrer, Austin. *A Study in St. Mark.* London, 1951.

Funk, Robert W. *Language, Hermeneutic and the Word of God.* New York, 1966.

Grant, R. M. *A Short History of the Interpretation of the Bible.* London, 1965.

Grobel, Kendrick. "Interpretation." In *The Interpreter's Dictionary of the Bible,* edited by G. A. Buttrick, II. New York, 1962.

Habel, Norman. *Literary Criticism of the Old Testament.* Philadelphia, 1971.

Harris, Victor. "Allegory to Analogy in the Interpretation of Scripture," *Philosophical Quarterly* 45 (1966): 1–23.

Henderson, Ian. *Myth in the New Testament.* London, 1952.

Jaspers, Karl. "Myth and Religion." In *Kerygma and Myth* 2. London, 1962.

Kerygma and Myth: A Theological Debate. London, 1972. (A single volume edition of *Kerygma and Myth,* vol. 1, 2nd ed., 1964, and vol. 2, 1962.) Edited by Hans-Werner Bartsch. Translated by Reginald Fuller.

Lampe, G. W. H., and Woollcombe, K. J. *Essays on Typology.* London, 1957.

Leach, E. R. *Genesis as Myth and Other Essays.* London, 1970.

Lubac, Henri de. *Exégèse médiévale: les quattre sens de l'Ecriture.* 4 vols. Paris, 1959–1964.

Macquarrie, John. *The Scope of Demythologizing: Bultmann and His Critics.* London, 1960.

Origen. *Contra Celsum.* Translated with an Introduction and Notes by Henry Chadwick. Cambridge, 1965.

Pannenberg, Wolfhart. *Theology and the Philosophy of Science.* Translated by Francis McDonagh. Philadelphia, 1976.

Preus, J. S. *From Shadow to Promise: Old Testament Interpretation from Augustine to Luther.* Cambridge, Mass., 1969.

Ramsey, Ian T. *Religious Language.* New York, 1963.

Robinson, J. M. "Hermeneutic Since Barth." In *The New Hermeneutic,* edited by J. M. Robinson and J. B. Cobb. New York, 1964.

Schmithals, Walter. *An Introduction to the Theology of Rudolf Bultmann.* Translated by John Bowden. London, 1968.

Smalley, Beryl. *The Study of the Bible in the Middle Ages.* 2nd ed. Oxford, 1952; Notre Dame, Ind., 1964.

Smart, J. D. *The Interpretation of Scripture.* London, 1961.

Via, Dan Otto, Jr. *The Parables: Their Literary and Existential Dimension.* Philadelphia, 1967.

Wilder, Amos N. *The Language of the Gospel: Early Christian Rhetoric.* New York, 1964.

Wolfson, H. A. *Philo: Foundations of Religious Philosophy in Judaism, Christianity and Islam.* 2nd ed. 2 vols. Cambridge, Mass., 1948.

Wood, J. D. *The Interpretation of the Bible: A Historical Introduction.* London, 1958.

5. Literary and Art Criticism

Auerbach, Erich. *Mimesis: The Representation of Reality in Western Literature.* Translated by W. R. Trask. Princeton, 1953.

———. "Figura." In *Scenes from the Drama of European Literature,* translated by Ralph Manheim. New York, 1959.

———. *Literary Language and Its Public in Late Latin Antiquity and in the Middle Ages.* Translated by Ralph Manheim. Princeton, 1965.

Barfield, Owen. *Poetic Diction: A Study in Meaning.* London, 1928. Reprint, New York, 1964.

———. "Poetic Diction and Legal Fiction." In *The Importance of Language,* edited by Max Black. Englewood Cliffs, N.J., 1962. (Originally in *Essays Presented to Charles Williams.* London, 1947.)

Barthes, Roland. *Elements of Semiology.* Translated by A. Lavers and C. Smith. London, 1967.

———. "Science versus Literature." In *Introduction to Structuralism,* edited by Michael Lane, pp. 410–416. New York, 1970.

Boas, George. *The Hieroglyphics of Horapollo.* New York, 1950.

Butler, Samuel. "Thought and Language," *Collected Essays,* vol. 2. New York, 1925. Also in *The Importance of Language,* edited by M. Black. Englewood Cliffs, N.J., 1962.

Charity, A. C. *Events and Their Afterlife: The Dialectics of Christian Typology in the Bible and Dante.* Cambridge, 1966.

Coleridge, S. T. *Biographia Literaria.* Edited by J. Shawcross. 2 vols. London, 1907.

Collingwood, R. G. *The Principles of Art.* Oxford, 1938.

Crane, R. S. *The Languages of Criticism and the Structure of Poetry.* Toronto, 1953.

Culler, Jonathan. *Structuralist Poetics: Structuralism, Linguistics and the Study of Literature.* London, 1975.

Dunbar, H. F. *Symbolism in Medieval Thought*. New Haven, 1929.

Empson, William. *Seven Types of Ambiguity*. 3rd ed. New York, 1955.

Fletcher, Angus. *Allegory: The Theory of the Symbolic Mode*. Ithaca, 1964.

Frye, Northrop. *Anatomy of Criticism*. Princeton, 1957.

Galden, J. A., S. J. "Typology and Seventeenth-Century Literature." Dissertation, Columbia University, 1965.

Gardner, Helen. *The Business of Criticism*. Oxford, 1959.

Gombrich, E. H. *Art and Illusion*. New York, 1960.

Hart, Ray L. *Unfinished Man and the Imagination*. New York, 1968.

Hollander, Robert B., Jr. *Allegory in Dante's Commedia*. Princeton, 1969.

Honig, Edwin. *Dark Conceit*. Evanston, Ill., 1959.

Hopper, S. R., and Miller, D. L., eds. *Interpretation: The Poetry of Meaning*. New York, 1967.

Huxley, Aldous. "Words and Their Meanings." In *The Importance of Language,* edited by M. Black. Englewood Cliffs, N.J., 1962.

Kahler, Erich. *The Inward Turn of Narrative*. Translated by R. and C. Winston. Princeton, 1973.

Langer, Susanne K. *Feeling and Form: A Theory of Art*. London, 1953.

Lawall, Sarah. *Critics of Consciousness: The Existential Structures of Literature*. Cambridge, Mass., 1968.

Lewalski, B. K. *Milton's Brief Epic*. Providence, R.I., 1966.

————. *Donne's Anniversaries and the Poetry of Praise: The Creation of a Symbolic Mode*. Princeton, 1973.

Lewis, C. D. *The Poetic Image*. London, 1947.

Lewis, C. S. "Bluspels and Flalansferes," *Rehabilitations and Other Essays*. London, 1929. Also in *The Importance of Language,* edited by M. Black. Englewood Cliffs, N.J., 1962.

Madsen, William. *From Shadowy Types to Truth*. New Haven, 1968.

Mazzeo, J. A. *Structure and Thought in the Paradiso*. Ithaca, 1958.

————. *Medieval Cultural Tradition in Dante's Comedy*. Ithaca, 1960.

Müller-Vollmer, Kurt. *Towards a Phenomenological Theory of Literature: A Study of Wilhelm Dilthey's Poetik*. The Hague, 1963.

Polletta, Gregory T., ed. *Issues in Contemporary Criticism*. Boston, 1973.

Robertson, D. W., Jr. *A Preface to Chaucer*. Princeton, 1962.

Rostow, Murray. *Biblical Drama in England*. Evanston, Ill., 1968.

Scholes, Robert. *Structuralism in Literature: An Introduction*. New Haven, 1974.

Spitzer, Leo. *Linguistics and Literary History: Essays in Stylistics*. Princeton, 1948.

Waismann, Friedrich. "The Resources of Language." In *The Importance of Language,* edited by M. Black. Englewood Cliffs, N.J., 1962.

Wellek, René. *Concepts of Criticism*. Edited by S. Nichols, Jr. New Haven, 1963.

———— and Warren, Austin. *Theory of Literature*. 3rd ed. New York, 1962.

Wheelwright, Phillip. *The Burning Fountain*. Bloomington, Ind., 1954.

6. Psychological Interpretation

Bachelard, Gaston. *The Psychoanalysis of Fire*. Translated by A. C. M. Ross. London, 1964.

Bodkin, Maud. *Archetypal Patterns in Poetry*. London, 1934.

Fliess, Robert. *Symbol, Dream and Psychosis*. New York, 1973.

Hoffman, Frederick J. *Freudianism and the Literary Mind*. Baton Rouge, 1945.

Jones, Ernest. "The Theory of Symbolism." In *Papers on Psychoanalysis*. 5th ed. 1948. Reprint New York, 1961.

Kris, Ernst. *Psychoanalytic Explorations in Art*. New York, 1952.

Kubie, Lawrence S. *Neurotic Distortion of the Creative Process*. Lawrence, Kans., 1958. Reprint New York, 1961.

Rapaport, David, trans. and ed. *Organization and Pathology of Thought*. New York, 1951.

Ricoeur, Paul. *Freud and Philosophy: An Essay in Interpretation*. Translated by D. Savage. New Haven, 1970.

Royce, J. R., ed. *Psychology and the Symbol*. New York, 1965.

Sharpe, E. F. *Dream Analysis*. London, 1937.

Spector, Jack J. *The Aesthetics of Freud: A Study in Psychoanalysis and Art*. New York, 1972.

Werner, H., and Kaplan, B. *Symbol Formation*. New York, 1963.

7. Scientific Interpretation

Beament, J. W. L., ed. *Models and Analogues in Biology*. Cambridge, 1960.

Braithwaite, R. B. *Scientific Explanation*. New York, 1953. Reprint New York, 1960.

Canguilhem, Georges. "The Role of Analogies and Models in Biological Discovery." In *Scientific Change,* edited by H. C. Crombie. New York, 1963.

Ghiselin, M. T. *The Triumph of the Darwinian Method*. Berkeley 1969.

Hesse, Mary B. *Models and Analogies in Science*. Notre Dame, Ind., 1966.

Kuhn, Thomas S. *The Structure of Scientific Revolutions*. 2nd ed. Chicago, 1970.

Leatherdale, W. H. *The Role of Analogy, Model and Metaphor in Science*. New York, 1974.

Rousseau, G. S., ed. *Organic Form: The Life of an Idea*. London, 1972.

Thom, René. *Stabilité structurelle et morphogenèse: Essai d'une théorie générale des models*. Reading, Mass., 1972.

Thompson, D'Arcy Wentworth. *On Growth and Form*. 2 vols. 2nd ed. Cambridge, 1942.

———. *On Growth and Form*. Abridged edition, edited by John Tyler Bonner. Cambridge, 1961.

Index